W9-BXU-292

Other books by the same author

Fitzgo: The Wild Dog of Central Park

You Don't Have to Be Rich to Own a Brownstone
(*with Joy Wilkes*)

THESE PRIESTS STAY

PAUL WILKES

simon and schuster
new york

Published by Simon and Schuster
Rockefeller Center, 630 Fifth Avenue
New York, New York 10020

SBN 671-21677-5
Library of Congress Catalog Card Number: 73-16477
Manufactured in the United States of America
1 2 3 4 5 6 7 8 9 10

My thanks to you priests who shared your doubts and faith with me. Some of your words are here to touch others. Know that I first and most deeply have been touched by your harsh and dreadful love.

To all those women and men
who will make the priesthood of believers
a reality

Contents

Introduction

The figures vary, depending on the source,* but it is a safe estimate that 15 per cent of American Roman Catholic priests have resigned since the Second Vatican Council. That leaves 85 per cent intact—presumably. Among those are the halt and the lame, either physically or mentally, plus various categories of men who feel they are too old or ill-trained to leave and those so enveloped in the arms of Holy Mother Church that they are afraid to depart. Also included, and composing, I hope, the majority, are functioning priests.

Ever since large-scale defections (resignations? laicizations?) began in 1964, the very fact of men leaving the priesthood has fostered great interest in the press and has produced any number of books

* An accurate figure is impossible to obtain, but a responsible estimate was obtained through this circuitous route: The Vatican's Central Statistical Office of the Church noted that 13,440 priests worldwide formally left between 1964 and 1970. This works out to a yearly rate of about 0.5 per cent. Worldwide, the defection rate among diocesan clergy was 6.6 per thousand, but in the United States it was 15 per thousand, or more than double. That would put the rate of United States priests leaving at more than 1 per cent a year. After Rome released the figures, Vatican observers said they would add at least another 30 per cent to take into account those priests who left without formal application.

—books of compassion and heartbreak, axe-grinding books, survey books. This particular book addresses itself to the men who have stayed. Let me quickly add that I am not talking about those perennial adolescents in Roman collars who would be intimidated by having to pay their own electric bill or sending their own clothes to the cleaners or men so unsure of themselves that the Astrodome of the church is the only place they are comfortable.* Because of contact first with a priest friend and then with a larger number of priests, I came to realize that there are a significant number of men who have given serious thought to leaving the priesthood but who have stayed. What brought them to the priesthood, what brought them to the verge of leaving it, and what causes them to remain priests are what this book is about. It is not a survey; it is composed of the words of real people and not statistics.

It is not so shocking that the good American boys who became good American priests would have severe doubt about their work in this drastically changed church. After all, they were raised and schooled in an era when the church was powerful, all-knowing. To be accepted into a seminary in the 1940s and even through the early 1960s brought inestimable pride to a home. To be ordained a priest was almost a coronation. The respect shown to a priest was unrivaled in the small world in which mid-century Catholics moved. Many priests had successfully filled their roles, but when the rules were changed and they were told to be themselves and also be priests, it was too much. Still others found that their love—Holy Mother Church—had become a whore mother and they could no longer face the contradictions. They said, over and over again as they left, We can no longer live a lie.

What many of today's priests saw in the 1940s was still an im-

* "The Loyola Psychological Study of the Ministry and Life of the American Priest," by Father Eugene Kennedy showed a shockingly small number of priests had developed to what psychologists consider "the adulthood stage." In one study only 19 out of 271 had reached this stage; in another study 11 out of 218 had achieved it.

migrant church whose ghetto mentality effectively curtailed lively intellectual or theological talk but which provided the security that ethnic groups in America still seemed to want. The church was the Catholics' country club, their educational institution, therapist, recreation director. The church was the Catholics' "turf," a sanctuary, the one place in a WASPish America where they were infinitely correct, where they knew they had an exclusivity that none of the heathen Protestants, Jews, or non-believers could share.

Along with most of the priests in this book I was a product of Catholic provincialism. When people asked me what section of my home city of Cleveland, Ohio, I lived in, I would never say the East Side or the Buckeye Road area. I would proudly and unabashedly say, "St. Benedict's parish." If they didn't know where that was, they surely didn't know where anything was. Our priests were Benedictines, and although we saw that they drank Budweiser and Black and White scotch while men like my father, a carpenter, were drinking P.O.C. and Corby's, and we knew that the priests were given to fits of ill will (not granting absolution after our confessing some sin against the sixth commandment), we never questioned that they might be putting something over on us. That Father Leo and Father Michael and all those men with their comfortable bellies pushing out their black habits never did talk much about Christ's love or our need to spread it didn't bother us at all. The bazaar was coming up and Mom had to start making cakes for the booths and my six brothers and sisters and I had to sell chances on the Pontiac that was to be given away on the final night.

St. Benedict's was the fixed point in a changing world and we were happy to have it, to have priests who possessed the fullness of doctrine and who could, as I would later draw a parallel while serving in the Navy, solve any problem, answer any question with the finality and completeness of a Department of Defense directive. We were brainwashed to believe that these priests did have the fullness of Christian thought. In their seminary training, in turn, they had been first hazed, then indoctrinated, and then given elaborate proofs and defenses that they could recite word for word so they could become "defenders of the faith."

Roles were clearly defined for lay people and priests at St. Benedict's and at churches throughout America. Our parents were supposed to send us to Catholic schools; various members of the family were supposed to attend church activities from Holy Name to Altar Society, get baskets blessed at Easter, do right by meat and labor on appointed days, get to church on Sundays and holy days, and participate in the most magnificent liturgical event of the year, the church bazaar. We were supposed to give until it hurt, chip in for those second collections that seemed to come every week that sent money to the Pope or foreign missions or to agencies that would propagate the faith in the pagan areas of our own United States. At year's end a little booklet, printed on high-gloss enamel paper, would be distributed, listing the donations of each member of every family. The thinking must have been that if you hadn't been giving until it hurt, it was going to hurt then.

If the role of the laity was defined, that of the priest was even more defined. He was first a cultic high priest who officiated in a foreign language, Latin, which, because we could not understand it, we thought surely must be ordained by God and obviously above those of us who sat in the pews. Priests were supposed to sit and read in the rectory, be available to give the last sacraments to the dying, but not be so available that any of us would dare stop by for a visit. All our personal problems could be discussed in the confessional; our personal thoughts could be kept to ourselves. After all, what could we offer these learned men? Priests would also give us a catechism lesson weekly, hand out report cards, oversee the various parish groups, sponsor a youth group or coach a football team. Seeing Father Louis in a sweat suit and football shoes for the first time was like seeing Queen Elizabeth in jeans and sneakers. When one of my grade school classmates, Paul Forgach, joined the Benedictines and walked to the monastery a few hundred yards from the school, it was as if he was transported into another world, a more perfect one from which he would never return. He would be a priest for life, nobody doubted that.

The ideal priest was one who could say a six o'clock Mass in under twenty minutes so the golfers could get out to the course early, who could visit old people and distribute communion with some degree of kindness, and who didn't let his humanity show too much so that the laity might think that there was a day, long ago, when he was one of them. The faithful priest merely had to stay, he didn't need to inspire. An ideal pastor paid off mortgages in record time. Bishops were not spiritual leaders but construction engineers. Cardinal McIntyre was known as a "brick and mortar" man—a high accolade indeed—and at one point was building a new church every sixty-six days and a new school every twenty-six days in his boomland in Los Angeles. He was an admired man, a modern saint.

The immigrant's son or grandson, coming from a home rich in ethnic charm but lacking in Western culture, could see that by becoming a priest he could rise to a stratum virtually unreachable through any other means. Boys from common homes, often from large families, would go away to a magnificent stone seminary set off by trimmed lawns and trees and flowers and emerge seven years later as men of knowledge, intellectuals by the community's standards. In retrospect the church found, after Vatican II, it had created Frankenstein monsters. The church had taught these common men to reason, and with that power many of them could no longer reckon with the church's contradictions and they reasoned themselves right out of the priesthood.

After World War II, because of the G.I. Bill, great numbers of lay Catholics were also exposed to higher education. In turn, these college graduates became more discerning church members, questioning their professional managers (the priests) about education, parish affairs, and other sacred preserves of the clergy. Catholics, long the "silent Americans," also began to move out of their ghettos and into the larger society, and they started the ferment in the church that was to come to fruition in Vatican II.

As laity power increased, the power of the priest slowly began to be eroded. Slowly, it must be underscored, for the decades of clerical supremacy and lay dependency were not likely to blow away, no matter how strong the winds of change. That Senator Joseph McCarthy (a Catholic and a graduate of the same university, Marquette, at which I did time) would be held up as a model Catholic and congratulated by cardinals and prayed for by schoolchildren was a sign that American Catholics were desperately trying to be recognized in the nation that had for so long shunned them.

Even though the 1950s marked the emergence of a more questioning lay Catholic, those years were also a boom era for the church. New parishes were built as suburban areas grew. Huge schools went up to house the children of the faithful, and seminaries were built or expanded to house the increasing number of men who wanted to study for the priesthood.

Meanwhile, a number of men were writing about a new, prophetic role for the church and the need for pluralism in this, the oldest dictatorship on earth. In the 1940s and 1950s their books often were not well circulated; in some dioceses they were banned. Americans like John Courtney Murray, Europeans like Yves Congar, Henri de Lubac and Karl Rahner quietly went about their work as the tide of Catholic popularity seemed to indicate they were toiling in vain. It was only in 1958 when an unknown stubby Italian cardinal was chosen the "interim Pope" (until the current Pope, Paul VI, was ready for the office) that the church entered into an era of self-reflection that would lead to a corporate crisis of faith and great numbers of men leaving the priesthood.

When John XXIII called the Second Vatican Council, which

met for four successive autumns beginning in 1962, there was little concern in the church. What could be lost? Conversions, vocations, churches, schools were being added yearly. Even Pope John, who surely saw need for reform, did not expect to see the church changed substantially from the one he had known for seventy years.

Vatican II was a kind of Rosemary's baby. Its essential thrust ended up being that church doctrine and practices could be questioned. A crack appeared in the dam.

Yet, many bishops came away from Vatican II as they had come away from other large church meetings, confident that whatever was adopted it would have little effect on their fiefdoms. But once the word was out and began to be interpreted throughout the world, priests began to realize that there was a new era dawning. Some priests greeted the changes happily, ready to shed conventions and restrictions. Some older priests, but mostly younger men, found that they had signed their names years ago to a contract that was still binding although much of the wording had been changed.

The hermetically sealed capsule of the church—which protected the person with a sacrament soon after birth, through to a blessed gravesite—had been burst and many Catholics didn't know if they liked the new air. Their priests and bishops had formerly shaped their history; they, in turn, had learned their apologetics well and were defenders of the True Faith. To keep that faith pure they were used to avoiding all contacts with Protestantism. Now they were handed a new rule book, and many of the pages were blank, to be filled in by the holder. They were being told that Protestants were not as error-ridden as once believed. They were told that their consciences would have to be consulted in many cases instead of running to Father for the answer.

Vatican II made it easier for men to leave the priesthood, and beginning in 1964 they did so in great numbers. Any number would be great when the comparison figure was virtually zero. Priests who left before the Council were few in number and their departure was always silent and thereafter undiscussed. Perhaps the most astounding revelation about priests that came to American Catholics after the Council was that their "men of God" were no better or worse than a cross section of other professional men. There were a few very good priests, a few terrible ones, and the vast majority in between. Priests were a reflection of Everyman, with Everyman's problems, his doubts about his life, career, and worth.

The exodus from the priesthood was accelerated in 1968 when Pope Paul VI, going against a group of experts he had commissioned, made an uncompromising statement condemning artificial birth control in his encyclical *Humanae Vitae*. Even conservative churchmen were surprised by the unyielding tone of the document. Middle-of-the-road clergy and lay people were dismayed. The supposed new church was already retrenching. *Humanae Vitae* may, as church history is written, be an even more powerful force than the Council. For what *Humanae Vitae* did, once and for all, was put to death the possibility of the Pope (and then his bishops) ruling by fiat. Never again would the Pope be able to proclaim and find his priests and bishops in line and ready to promulgate the word. From *Humanae Vitae* on, churchmen, both clergy and lay, would look at papal pronouncements in a new light. If he could be so wrong there, where else might he be in fault? seemed to sum up the feeling.

Without doubt the priesthood has changed more in these past ten years than any other ten years in church history. There is much more freedom for priests, given the serfdom that most had to put up with before from their superiors—pastors, or bishops. Still the power of the hierarchy is not as diffuse as some would like to believe. A bishop can still make an errant priest pay handily for stepping out of line. Reports appear weekly in the Catholic press about priests being suspended for various acts of disobedience or lack of adherence to liturgical forms. Still, the hierarchy is under critical attack. Andrew Greeley, a priest and a respected sociologist, spent two years studying the American priesthood and pronounced his scathing verdict in "Priests in the United States: Reflections on a Study." Greeley said, "I believe the present leadership of the church to be morally, intellectually and religiously bankrupt."

Amidst the tumult and the "earthquake" of the past ten years many American priests—the foot soldiers in the Army of Christ—looked at themselves, their work—and went AWOL. Still others, afraid to look, clung more firmly to the bosom of the church, comforted even though the flesh seemed to be a bit colder than they had remembered. Thousands of men (a Gallup poll showed that 23 per cent had considered leaving) went through the painful processes of reconsideration, some had their crisis of faith, their nervous breakdown, their affair with a woman. They saw the other side, the secular life, and they considered it, and yet they chose to stay. And in this book they tell why.

A look at the figures and projections shows them to be in a hardly popular career. With the huge numbers of priests who were ordained in the 1930s now coming up for retirement, resignations of other priests showing no signs of abating, and seminary enrollment half of what it was five years ago and the quality of seminarians noticeably lower, the outlook is bleak. By the end of this decade America's Catholics may be served by only half the number of men who were in the priesthood when the Council began.

The research for this book was not a survey, so I cannot present statistics or tables to the reader. What I can give from contacts with over a hundred priests are some predispositions, reflections, and problems that recurred in my conversations with these men. Some of these recurring items—fanciful and profound—can be noted in the words of the ten men I have selected for the book.

Pre-seminary: Many of the priests lived physically close to a church and attended Mass frequently if not daily. Almost all were products of Catholic schools. Many priests came from large families that were religiously inclined but not given to fanatic practices. There was little pressure at home for them to become priests. Quite a few felt a real call, a vocation to the priesthood.

Seminary: Except for young men who were escaping from an extremely repressive home situation, seminary usually was an unpleasant experience. Seminarians, most often on the East Coast, were treated inhumanely, yet the majority feel their education was a good one. Seminary rules against "particular friendships" seemed to have encouraged homosexuality rather than deterred it as the rules intended.

Once ordained: The diocesan priest assigned to a parish seemed to be confronted by one of two types of pastors, benign or dictatorial. The benign pastor let the curate chart his own path, get involved, and, within reason, improvise. The dictatorial pastor had rules about visitors in the priest's room, the hours he would keep, the topics of his sermons.

If any, there was only a minute amount of support available to a priest from the other men who lived with him in the rectory or community house. He usually tried to talk things through with his classmates, but often it was difficult to get together with them because of conflicting schedules. Priests who went through seminaries in the 1960s, when the spirit of community was being stressed, found little or none of the communitarian ethic present once they arrived at their assignments.

Once ordained, obtaining a car was quite important. The car appeared to represent some tangible object they could own, and also it proved to be an escape vehicle by which they could get away from the unpleasantness of job or fellow priests; it represented a sanctuary and freedom.

After being in a parish or teaching job for a short time, many younger priests found the work stifling and uncreative; they talked about wanting new ministries that they could carve out for themselves.

Discovering themselves: Virtually none of the men understood what the vow of celibacy was about, and most are angry that it was foisted upon them in their innocence. Very few see any merit in celibacy today. All would like to see celibacy made optional.

Through individual or group therapy or various sorts of sensitivity training, they came to grips with themselves as people and began to focus on the problems they were having as priests. This usually led to a painful period of reappraisal and reconsideration of the priesthood. Setting aside the role of priest and accepting himself as person seemed crucial.

Women and marriage: Women are almost always mentioned as being important at one stage or another in their lives. Many said they had "found love" as ordained priests. All are celibate; few have been entirely chaste. Women will continue to play a part in their lives; they are not afraid to become involved with a woman and do not see this as the first step out of the priesthood. None is eager to have his relationship with a particular woman a public matter.

The desire to marry immediately (if the celibacy law were relaxed) was stressed by very few men. Sex is not the overpowering element in most priests' lives. Either they feel comfortable and enjoy the company of women (most do) or else they have, for a variety of reasons, displaced their sexuality into something else—work or material objects—or have entirely sublimated it.

Possibility of leaving: Loneliness was the chief problem cited for men who considered leaving. They felt they had no one with whom to share their triumphs and failures. The desire to marry is usually the reason why most priests leave, but loneliness brought them to that point.

After loneliness, authority was the most often mentioned problem area. Young priests especially feel they have little to say in the rectory, order or diocese. For the most part they are unimpressed with the quality of leadership, citing the preponderance of "company men" who get the best jobs and the conviction that that has perpetuated poor leadership.

The years 1968 and 1969 seemed to contain a "crisis of faith" for many of the men.

This book is arbitrarily divided into three sections, and the ten men have been placed under headings that seem to be central to why they thought of leaving the priesthood. The areas are insensitivity, authority, and sex. The words of each man as they appear in this book were obtained through extensive tape-recorded interviews that were then edited down for clarity and to make each a manageable size. All the priests have had a chance to review their material to make corrections and to give additional clarification where they thought necessary.

Finding a good number of priests who would honestly come forward and say they had questioned whether they could stay in the priesthood was a rather laborious chore that was aided by people too numerous to mention here. I had to go to friends, priests, journalists, and professional organizations in my quest. I thank those nameless hordes who helped me so much.

Tribute is due to Bertha Hoopes, who patiently transcribed the thousands of pages of interviews, and to Louise Fisher, who quickly, professionally, and with good humor typed the manuscript and its revisions. Also I thank Joy Wilkes, my wife, a woman of intelligence, patience, and love, who is not only a wonderful life's companion but a fine editor.

Brooklyn, New York
September, 1973

part one

The Church of Stone: Insensitivity

"The headlines were screaming, the coverage was distorted, so I wrote a long letter to all the priests in the archdiocese, trying to tell them what had happened and why. Not only was there no support, but some priest gave the letter to a cop in his parish. . . . This letter got to the mayor and I was arrested for inciting to riot."

—Father Jack McCaslin

"I guess this was symbolic of the troubles that would follow. Here was a day that could have been made very special. The bishop talked to me like a child, saying that I hadn't gotten permission, and his voice said he was very angry with me. 'I have a mind not to let anybody receive under both species.' "

—Father Charles Tobin

"We had put a lot of emphasis on community in the last years in the seminary, and I could see communal strength as something that would support me in my work. . . . I came out thinking rectories were pretty much the same. I guess I was naïve enough to think that priests actually were automatically very charitable and kind and that there was a fraternal community in every rectory."

—Father Richard Martin

Father Jack McCaslin

Father Jack McCaslin's parish, Holy Family, is in Omaha's once proud but now crumbling North Side where the demolition of houses has left many blocks looking like the mouths of old men who have lost most of their teeth. But inside Holy Family Church, which he serves as pastor, sunlight shines through old-style stained glass on banners that read "Color My World with Hope" and "People Are Like Kites, Meant to Be Raised Up." The alcove where cherubs, angels, and saints once watched over a marble altar is now painted over. Simple, rough house siding is now the backdrop for the table that serves as an altar.

Inside his small crowded office Jack McCaslin sits, with a Martin Luther King poster keeping a steady gaze on him from the wall, a wall where peeling wallpaper has been unceremoniously and sloppily put back in place. He is forty-three, has a trimmed beard, and, like most men who have staked their claims in the decaying parts of cities, would never have anyone guessing his age younger than it is.

Jack McCaslin thumbs his way through the checkbook receipts. A family's gas bill came to $99.75. A bed was purchased for $20. A check for $375 was made out to the grocery store for food pur-

chased for needy families. A ticket to Denver for a runaway to get back home cost $19.75. He comes to a check for $26.25 for parish envelopes. "Now there's someplace we have to cut back."

Jack McCaslin knows poverty, but if there was such a thing during the Depression, he knew a "poverty with dignity" of a Catholic family with thirteen children. In back of the McCaslin home in Omaha was a huge garden through which Jack's father pushed a one-wheeled plow. McCaslin children swarmed over the garden picking off potato bugs. Poor as they were, the McCaslins always had a little bit to share with those even less fortunate, so the service to the poor that Jack practiced as a seminarian came naturally.

He leaped into the priesthood, a zealot for Christ, misdirected at times but terribly sincere and terribly hard-working. He preached and talked privately about the evils of boys and girls in parked cars; he attacked television as something that would kill the family. But he also preached for fair wages and unions.

Considering himself already somewhat of an avant-garde priest because of the innovations he fostered in liturgy and issues he confronted, Jack McCaslin was himself confronted by the Vatican Council in 1963. It shook him to his roots. He studied the new theology and, after a period of agonizing over this body of new thoughts, found it said something to him, something fresh, something he had to put into practice. He was then in rural Nebraska and fellow priests turned him off, refused to give him support.

This sent Jack McCaslin back to the city, where he thought the new Gospel must be not only taught but lived out. With a handful of people he organized what turned out to be weak demonstrations, but he found himself called the "Groppi of Omaha." He was called an anarchist and found himself out of favor with the archbishop and about to be exiled to a neutral ground where he could spend a year or so at school cooling off.

Condemned by fellow priests, laymen, newspapers, Jack McCaslin reached a point where he had to decide if the things he wanted to accomplish couldn't be done more effectively outside the church.

It's hard to sort it all out. I can think of a toilet-paper box full of letters protesting what I was doing with the inner city people of Omaha. I can think of driving my car out of town and parking alongside the road and just crying. Then there were the four days in the hospital, total physical and emotional exhaustion, when I wondered how I could go on as a priest. I knew I couldn't leave the church, but the priesthood? Why stay? Let me go way back to my childhood, the seminary, my parishes, my experiences, and see if I can put some of the pieces together.

We were a financially poor family, but we were never culturally poor. Our house was a fun place with all of those kids—thirteen of them—and the young priests from our parish, Holy Angels, came one after another. The pastor was an old Irish tyrant, and the young priests escaped to our place. We sang a lot, and we didn't have a radio or anything like that.

Mass was always a big thing for me. I am sure that since I was seven I have gone to Holy Communion 80 per cent of the days. Rosary wasn't a big thing in the family except during the war when my brother Tom was at the front.

It's hard to figure out where all those vocations in my family came from. Five priests and one nun. Nobody was a holy-holy. We were all athletic, but we were all little runts, except for my brother Dick, who was a real star baseball player. And I guess we were tough kids too. We grew up tough. And scrap, scrap intensively. In fact, we were kind of the devils of the neighborhood. A lot of the neighborhood thought those McCaslin kids would never come to anything.

One Halloween we painted the bottom half of one lady's white house brown. She never did like us much, maybe because we were

Catholics. She had a big hog in her back yard, and the next Halloween we decided we would let her hog out. But she was waiting in pitch blackness for us. My poor brother Dick nearly got beaten to death with a mop or a broom or whatever she was swinging at him. I finally had to vault back over the fence, grab the broom, and push Dick over to rescue him.

I worked construction in the summer and I learned all the cuss words. But beneath all the roughness, religion meant a lot. I used to practice saying Mass as a little kid. I knew the Our Father in Latin at a terribly early age. I was the priest's helper, and any time another guy didn't show up to serve Mass they knew they could get McCaslin. The nuns used to have me clean out those vigil lights and other stuff.

I don't remember now what was the attraction, but I never wanted to be anything but a priest. You know, most kids grow up wanting to be a fireman, but I never wanted to be anything but a priest. I had a vision of priests and I had a sense of needing to serve.

The pastor used to come to our house frequently. He drank too much and we knew it. He was of the old Irish tyrant school. He golfed too much and he cussed at us even when we caddied for him. On the altar we would make mistakes and he really was hard on us—that was worse. But you know, when the assistants would come over and talk about P. A.—that's what everyone called him, P. A.—and his Cadillac convertible, my ma would cut that off: "Now we don't talk about priests in this house." I didn't think priests went to the toilet like the rest of human beings, things like that. The image of the priesthood was terribly high; it was only later that I learned they had faults. But then most of the priests who came were outstanding young guys, like Father Beuhler, who was around the longest in my growing-up years. That man walked around that parish day after day for years, seeing to the needs of the people.

As poor as we were, my ma sewed and gathered secondhand clothing for a poor family in Petersburg that Father Beuhler had found. Then there was a little old lady we called the little vanilla lady—she sold vanilla extract, cold cream, and stuff—who lived down in a little old trailer with a lot of cats and dogs at the bottoms, as we called it, of the river. The river flooded about every spring and she would come up to live at our house, and we didn't even have enough room for ourselves. On Thanksgiving, when we were struggling for ourselves, there was always a basket for the vanilla lady.

I really don't remember all the specifics, but the notion of helping the poor really rang, because when I came home from seminary in the summer I got involved with the Martin de Porres Club here that worked with blacks and poor people, and when I went to Catholic University I worked in the slums for four years in Washington. At Conception seminary after World War II I was the head of a group who sent packages to Austria and Germany. We always put a bottle of lard in there—they used it for butter—and secondhand clothing that people gave us.

In high school girls entered the picture, and that is why I entered the seminary in my senior year. I really thought I ought to be a priest, but suddenly the fellows that I ran around with were becoming alive to girls, and sports were becoming a little less important.

Ma fell into a little inheritance, $4,000, from an uncle, and I asked her if it was possible to dip in for $450 for me to go away to Conception Abbey in Missouri. My folks didn't like the idea much. They said I was too young and I really didn't know what I wanted to do. But I persisted and never told them I was afraid that I was running around with all of these guys who were going to be running with girls and that this might endanger my vocation. It was very real. Immature, but it was very real.

I was very interested in girls, you see, and I remember an incident where brother Jim—he eventually went into the priesthood—had a girl friend who had a girl friend who didn't have a date, and we were just going to a movie or something. And I said, Yeah, I'll do it. But as the time drew closer and closer I got cold feet and didn't go. It would have been a very heavy thing for me to do. I mean I kind of liked the idea. And that scared me.

So I went to Conception Abbey, which is forty miles this side of St. Joe, Missouri, the place where all those great cards and posters come out of now. And all of a sudden I was swept up in this magnificently progressive place which was then a center for liturgical reform, a place full of teachers who could show loving concern. The spiritual life was very liturgically and community oriented. The Mass and the breviary were in English, then we would pray in Latin, sing Gregorian chants, and the whole thing was tremendously attractive to me. Five beautiful growing years. We ate in the monastery and after supper we walked down the long monastic hallways and went to the abbey church where Rosary and Stations of the Cross were said privately for those who wished.

There were none of the strict rules we heard about in other seminaries. Conception's rules took up one page. They didn't want liquor in the rooms. Visiting was allowed, only you couldn't cross the threshold. Those were exciting years, 1946–1951, terribly exciting years of Catholic Action clubs, the Jocist's technique, Young Christian Students, Young Christian Workers, Christian Family Movement, group cell things, Dorothy Day, Peter Maurin, and the Catholic Worker movement.

The mystical body of Christ was a doctrine which had died with St. Augustine or somebody hundreds of years before, and now Pius XII wrote the encyclical *Mystici Corporis,* which talked about the mystical body of Christ and said that we all have a part to play. The Benedictines at Conception took that very seriously and worked at it. The Christian Family Movement was coming into our lives. There was a great feeling that the new monster television was going to destroy family community. I told my folks if they got a television set I wasn't coming home.

I had asked to go back to Conception for the four years of theology, but instead in 1951 I went to Catholic U. That place was the antithesis of the life I had been experiencing. At Catholic U we said the Rosary out loud and sang "On This Day, Oh, Beautiful Mother," and here I had come from a progressive liturgical atmosphere to this kind of stuff. We used to gather at five-thirty in the morning, or some ungodly hour, and sit in the prayer hall for meditating. At five-thirty in the morning I can't think, much less pray. Once or twice a week they would read a meditation at us. Gory stuff! Scourging at the pillar, talking about the whip and the flesh down on the ground.

The Sulpician Fathers were running the theological college, and great men and great seminary trainers they were, but it was a very strongly personalized rather than communitarian kind of thing. Agonize, mortify the senses. Happily they did instill the need for private prayer, while the Benedictines had taught me communitarian spirituality.

We had a rule book, and every year the rector went through it, explaining it, telling the same jokes, and it wasted three or four months of our evening instruction. There were rules about smoking and what time lights had to be put out, and then this "particular friendship" thing; you couldn't walk with the same guy twice, I suspect because they worried about homosexuality—evidence of which I never saw. That was inhuman. Because cliques and particular friendships were so discouraged, we older priests don't know how to relate to people very well.

But the compensation was Washington itself. I was opened up to a new world of art and music. Catholic U had big-name speakers coming in, and the political activity was really something that I dug. On Wednesday and Saturday afternoons we were free to join what we called "walks." I went to Freedman's General Hospital.

It was for TB patients, black people mostly, who had come up from the South, who had to get lungs removed. They needed thirteen pints of blood when they were going to do lung surgery, so I organized thirteen guys from Catholic U when the call came. There were other things going, like at Fides House and at the Peter Claver Center in the black ghettos with the poorest of the poor. We were painting, visiting, instructing, making converts, helping people clean up houses, moving furniture, using education programs, youth activities. I could put up with a whole gang of things because of those Wednesdays and Saturdays.

I think my serving at that time was very paternalistic; I was going to help the poor slobs who didn't know anything. I don't think during that time I really analyzed that there is a difference between financial poverty and cultural poverty, that those who are only financially poor don't have to be culturally poor. Maybe that's what was pushing me to work with them.

Through all those ups and downs at Catholic U I don't think I really had questions about staying in. What I did have doubts about was whether or not I could make it into priesthood in that crazy place. The saddest part of it was that I was a terribly good law observer. If the law said don't smoke I didn't smoke, yet you could smell smoke all over the place. There I was twenty-five years old knocking on the prefect's door and saying, "I need an eraser from Joe, could I go ask him for one?" That was just keeping us stupid little kids.

But I got through all that, and ordination day was at hand in 1955. Ordination day itself was not the moving experience that I had anticipated. I should explain that I was not a feeling person. I grew up in an Irish Catholic home, a loving home where I knew that I was loved, and I loved. But there weren't strong emotional manifestations of this. And then seminary taught, Catholic schools taught, that anger is a sin, that feelings were not really Christian. You know, hate—that will put you right in hell. Lust, watch out for that one. It all had been solidified and concretized. I pushed my feelings into a steel case which was busted open only four years ago when I went to St. Louis to a communications workshop. It was a spontaneous emotional reaction thing for four days, where they just pounded the hell out of me. My friends now talk about the pre–St. Louis and post–St. Louis me.

Back to ordination day. I remember it was a strong act of faith, and it was a strong intellectual commitment to Christ and the work that I would be called to do. But it was the first Mass that was the moving experience. Jim, my brother, was ordained in December of the preceding year, and Ed had been ordained since 1944, and Dick and Pat were one and two years into the seminary; so my priest brothers and the rest of the family were there. The liturgy came from my Conception Abbey days, and that first Mass remains to this day a tremendously moving thing. I can remember the vestments that I wore, the setting at Holy Angels Church, the Corpus Meum—"This is my body"—at the consecration. I also remember the physical pain of standing on that hard floor at the reception. My legs felt like they were crammed up into my body. I recall my inability to relate to people whom I had known all my life who were coming up and saying, "Hello, Father," while I wondered, What do I say back?

I think I was able to love then, but it was a love in Christ and always in the context of doing for and helping others. I describe it as kind of a brick wall with a barbed wire fence on top that went outward, so I'd go over all right, but nobody could get back in.

O.K., with whatever shortcomings I had, I was a priest. And in the five churches I would serve I ran the gamut from freedom to suppression, and also in the process I just had to change my theology completely and really come to grips with whether I could remain a Roman Catholic priest. One of my first churches was in a parish of Italians on Omaha's South Side; the pastor being a man ordained in Italy in 1930 or so. He told me that in American seminaries there were new things happening and this was no longer an Italian parish and he needed a young American guy with American ideas. He wanted me to feel free to use whatever I could to bring Christ to that parish. He was just fabulous.

I worked from early morning until late at night every day, walking door to door. In two years' time we fixed up twenty-eight bad marriages. We went from four poorly attended Masses to five very well attended Masses. I did a lot of crazy things. On First Friday, I would call a hundred families and say, "Tomorrow is First Friday and we've got a special thing. We're trying to get everybody out." And with that personal touch, they'd come.

There was a nurses' residence across the street. Their boy friends would come, and I'd see them sitting over there necking in the cars. At night, at about ten-thirty, I would go out—in cassock yet—and pray my Rosary walking around in the lot. Good heavens, the poor devils, what they needed was the presence of the cloth. This would give them strength, something to withstand all temptations to violate purity. But that didn't help; they just moved a little deeper into the parking lot. I used to walk up and down the sidewalk that bisected the lot, and when that didn't help I'd get into the car with them and talk to them. Very immature, but I was filled with a real, genuine zeal to draw people to Christ. They used to tell me, "You don't understand. You've never had a relationship." And I said I understood about sin. I knew that if they didn't have ice water in their veins they couldn't continue this very long without committing sin. All that served to do was to alienate me from student nurses whom I could have been a great influence on.

Two years went by in the parish and things were really building. I had brought in a lot of my ideas about liturgy and worship and participation and lay responsibility. But there was a new burgeoning area for a parish, which was in a better, quite rich, section, and I was assigned to it. The pastor was a young guy, a tremendous pastor, but he was jealous of his own authority. All the things like knocking on doors and just becoming friends with the people—I wasn't permitted to do that. The pastor ultimately would have been happy if I had just stayed in my room and done my assigned duties in the school and rectory.

The pastor didn't like what I preached either. I was preaching about unions, talking to wealthy people, asking them to pay just wages to their employees. Also I was on a kick about working on Sunday. Those people had big fancy lawns and crab grass, and Sunday was often their day to work outdoors. I was really very rigid about what kind of dress they should wear, about shorts that were too short, things like that that had to be considered, in my mind, if you were going to be a genuine Christian.

I was not happy, but I stuck it out for four years. It was a stifling atmosphere, but I did work hard. I would go out and bless the house of each new family. Often I would be out all day in 100-degree weather with the black suit and collar, sweating to death.

"Where the hell have you been? People have been calling you all day," the pastor would say. And I'd hand him this list, the census sheet, and say, "Here's where I've been, and I don't know where I'm going to be tomorrow at two o'clock." I wasn't allowed to stand in front of the church and greet people, because, he would say, "You can't because I can't." And I said, "If you could do all those things you wouldn't need an assistant." He was really a good man, a good pastor, just so insecure with an assistant.

But I never doubted the priesthood then. I think, growing up Irish and poor, I knew there were a lot of mountains to overcome; and every time a challenge came up, I'd say, Is it going to whip me or am I going to whip it? But after four years I went to the chancellor and said, "You have two guys working together, and it can be good if they work as a team. But we're not. We're working against each other."

So they transferred me, and I went to a church with a beautiful old pastor from Ireland. He left for vacation on a Thursday, and

I arrived there on Saturday. I didn't even know how to turn the lights on. He didn't come back until Labor Day, so I had the whole summer to myself. Things I had been dreaming about, like people singing in church and other community-building activities, I was able to do that summer. The people responded slowly but nicely and we were working toward building community. However, much of that was overturned when the pastor came back—not particularly because he was against it but because he didn't understand it and he just went his old way. He would celebrate Mass and not say the words loud enough so the people could respond to them. He had a thick Irish brogue which people could hardly understand, much less respond to.

The Liturgical Council had been started in 1941, and the whole notion of the mystical body was terribly important if anyone cared to read about it. I was reading *America, Commonweal, Jubilee, Worship,* and they helped keep me alive. The frustrating part of it was that the first three months had shown me that something could be done, progress could be made if I would just be let go. The pastor never really held me back, it was just that we always switched Masses, except the five-thirty Mass on Sunday (but at that hour we were all zombies; I couldn't do anything, and they couldn't either). The pastor would say the seven o'clock one week and the nine o'clock the next week. Any progress that I would make would be stopped, because he would mumble through the Mass and the people couldn't even say Amen.

In 1963 I was named pastor at Plainview, Nebraska, in a church of sixty-five families, with a mission at Brunswick with thirty-five families. Now all those things I had been thinking about and planning for and was frustrated in, I could begin. We set up committees and had monthly meetings. At the beginning they were just rubber stamps, but as time went by they took hold. Rural people already have much that makes a community out of them. Usually it centers around the public high school or just town loyalty. The idea is to take what's there and Christianize it. I worked for months talking about community worship, what being a Christian meant, loving one another. I hit hard at that.

Vatican II was on at this time and the first documents came out. The document on the liturgy was the first one that mattered to us, and every Sunday I took hunks of the document and explained it to them. I told the people that this was where the church was, that what I was telling them wasn't just coming from me.

I was there from 1963 to 1967. They were happy but painful years. In November of 1963 my first real crisis came. I thought I was the big avant-garde priest, and it came like a bolt that I was way behind the times. We had a four-day pastoral institute, with a scripture man, a sacramental theology man, a moral theology man, a catechism man, a sociologist, and a dogmatic theologian. I liked what I heard in those four days, but all it was was one big jumble. They gave us a bibliography and I bought exactly $209 worth of books and put myself on a reading schedule of three hours a day.

It was probably the most painful time I ever went through. For one thing, I was out of the studying habit. I kept trying to pour the new wine of existentialism into the old skins that I had learned in the seminary. I knew that I had to throw out a lot of my old theology if I was going to be preaching where the church was then. The only thing I was sure of was that Jesus came and love was what he came for. So every sermon was on love, and this went on for about six or eight months. It finally got to the people, and they would say, "Don't you think we've had enough of this love thing, Father?" And I said that they had to be patient with me until I could redirect my theology. I was sure of love, but I wasn't sure of much else. But I liked what I was hearing and reading. It was beautiful and it fit the way I felt the Christian message should be preached.

For instance, on Trinity Sunday. The Trinity that I had learned in the seminary and could spout off was all this business about the twenty-six processions—or whatever—that went on with God. But the new Trinitarian theology had very much to do with me. God loved me enough to send His son to reveal himself to me. The old theology had to do with somebody out there, and that didn't affect me so much, but the new stuff got awfully personal. I prayed like I'd never prayed before, because my faith was in jeopardy. I just didn't know what the hell I believed. I wanted to believe whatever the church was teaching, but I didn't know what the hell that was. I had known what the church was teaching before, because I was one of those teachers. I had gone through four years of theology and had studied hard to learn what that was. In 1963 I still had all the answers, which were just extended versions of the Baltimore Catechism, but that wasn't enough any more.

Then I found out that the Protestants had something, and we could learn from them. I found that much of our new theology really came from Bultmann, Tillich, and people like that. But the trauma that I went through in moving from my old seminary theology to the new was frightening. It wasn't a case of not believing, it was a case of wanting to believe but not knowing what to believe. Where was I? It cut my legs off, figuratively speaking, about where I was and about the sureness that I had about my faith. But I was fortunate again, because what I was hearing was very pleasant to my ear. What the new theology was doing was hacking away at the patness of everything, the sureness of everything. Man's relationship with God left a lot of unanswered things, man couldn't grasp God as readily as he thought.

I had plenty of books to read on the new theology, and that helped, but there I was in Plainview, Nebraska. What was more frustrating was that I was dealing with a deanery there. The deanery meetings consisted of the twelve priests of the area who got together with some regularity. I would try my new ideas on them, and I used to come home from those meetings with a big empty feeling. They were so steeped in the legalistic side; their faith was in the church and not in Christ. They would say, "This is the church's teaching"—or the Pope's or the bishop's. I would say that the church is everybody and that the Spirit is at work not just in the Pope and the bishops and the pastors, that He was at work in all people.

I drove them crazy because I did away with Baptism stipends, and Mass stipends didn't really matter to me. If people wanted me to remember them in Mass, that was fine. They would ask how much and I would tell them that it didn't cost anything.

Each deanery meeting was a great trauma, but I also felt that if we the priests couldn't put it together, how were we ever going to get the people put together? Only one other guy was somewhat with me, but he wasn't forceful. After I left he wrote, "I always admired you. I always felt bad that I didn't have the guts to join you. I agreed with you but I didn't always give you the support that I know you wanted." And I needed that support; boy, did I need it! I'm really not that smart, nor was I sure of my awakening position.

However, in Plainview and Brunswick we did develop Christian community. It wasn't like the world's greatest, and we were dealing with very conservative Nebraska farmers for the most part who didn't take to new things quickly. But things did change. The people came to some decision-making power, not just doing things because Father said so. When my successor came out, they told him, "We vote on things, Father." For instance, we had never made a permanent altar for the new liturgy. The man that followed me put up an expensive altar after the people had voted on a simple one. Well, it was just like a gigantic explosion heard all the way to the chancery office.

They began to involve themselves in Plainview, which in the past had been an anti-Catholic town. The Ku Klux Klan had been strong there in the 1920s and '30s, and there were remnants of that. No Catholic had ever run for office before, and then our Catholic druggist was elected to the City Council. When the National Farmers' Organization or the Swine Growers would come to town, people would put out bids—like the different churches and ladies' groups—to see who would serve them. They could make some money on that. Our ladies from the Altar Society had never bid, because they didn't think they would be acceptable. But they started doing that too.

These were simple beginnings of Christians participating in the life of the community. Also the Mass became more meaningful and the liturgy was a good experience. I could tell that in a number of ways. Coming to church was a happy experience, and the people weren't afraid to talk in church. It didn't matter if the kids cried or ran around in church. You could see parents' involvement in getting the kids to religious instruction and the kids wanting to be there. Also a guy who was giving a dollar a week started giving two dollars a week because he was more interested in the parish.

I saw progress in the people, but my own mind was unsettled. I wouldn't really have a crisis of faith until 1968, but I knew that my old cassock just didn't fit any more, and I didn't know what to put on. I didn't like the idea of being nude. Even in this struggle I think I was a good, effective rural pastor, but my heart was with the poor people in the city. When the job of director of social action opened up in Omaha, I went to see the archbishop. As it turned out, nobody else wanted the job, so I got it.

At that time marches and demonstrations were sweeping the country, but Omaha hadn't had anything. Groppi was marching up in Milwaukee at the time, so later thirty of us marched with him for open housing. When we got back we called a press conference and literally scared hell out of the whole city of Omaha and said that we were going to start doing the same kind of thing here. John Krejei was my assistant at the time and co-director of the social action office. We had a lot of marches and demonstrations and began to pressure landlords. We would stay outside rundown buildings until landlords promised that they would make the repairs. From the start we got guff from the bishop, from other priests, even from the blacks themselves—because some wanted to be king of the mountain too, and there was a lot of infighting, mainly because blacks were wanting to do for themselves. There was no shortage of flack from just about everybody, but we kept going.

In March of 1968 George Wallace came to town, and we planned a huge demonstration for his meeting. We were going to form a single line of marchers around the city auditorium with placards. By now we had learned to move out of the way and let the blacks take the lead, but it didn't work so well then because the young blacks led the procession and they marched right into the auditorium instead. I stayed with them and eventually the police let about fifty of them down on the floor, but the cops wouldn't let me go with them. So there were these blacks, militant as hell, making noise, but with essentially no leadership, either black or white.

As it turned out, this was just the thing to get votes for Wallace in no uncertain terms. It was just perfect staging for it: the hot room, the antagonizing wait for Wallace to appear, the itchy kids. Wallace delayed and delayed, and the Wallaceites were needling the kids. I was just about ready to collapse I was so exhausted, so I thought I'd better leave while I could still walk. I thought the point had been made.

In the middle of the night I was awakened by Father Krejei. He told me the kids were all down at the police station, that off-duty cops had come on like Black Shirts when Wallace came on and they took all the placards from the kids and the kids naturally protested. The cops moved in and Maced them all, then forced them to run a gauntlet where the people could hit them with metal folding chairs. It was a massacre. When these high school and college-age kids got out and mopped the blood and Mace off their faces, they began breaking car windows. Then the cops swept down, really bloodied them and arrested them.

The next morning the mayor issued a statement about how

awful we were and that the police did exactly the right thing to the kids in handling this "anarchy." So Krejei and I told the mayor that this was not the right thing to say, that these kids were mad, and that Omaha was going to have fires and riots unless he said some reasonable things. The mayor screamed at me that I was the instigator of the whole thing, and I said that was plain foolishness and that the cops had deliberately set up those kids to make them look bad.

The headlines were screaming, the coverage was distorted, so I wrote a long letter to all the priests in the archdiocese, trying to tell them what had happened and why. Not only was there no support, but some priest gave the letter to a cop in his parish. In the letter I gave the view of police brutality from the black side and I told about the rumors of police payoffs down in the black part of town and what the blacks thought about the cops. I made it clear I didn't know if there were payoffs, but the blacks thought there were.

This letter got to the mayor and I was arrested for inciting to riot. I was fingerprinted and booked. But they let me go on my own recognizance, though I was and still am a suspected criminal for writing that letter.

Then it really started. Something like four thousand letters sent either to the archbishop or to me, talking about the "nigger-loving bastard" and signed "Christian." The Archbishop had me out twice and I tried to explain where it was with the blacks and how as Christians and Catholics we had failed to address ourselves to the problem in the past, and we were now reaping the fruits of this. It was clear as a bell to me where Christ would have been if he were in Omaha in 1968. Meanwhile the mayor was asking the archbishop if there wasn't an Indian reservation somewhere that he could send McCaslin to.

And the archbishop was giving strong consideration to moving me out of town. I told him whether I did right or wrong was beside the point. It was the church and these were legitimate needs. You build new high schools and spend millions out in the suburbs and you close the inner city schools, I laid it out. Another pastor at an inner city church built a $750,000 basketball court. Big deal. This generation we make black basketball stars; we used to make them into boxers. Stop handing out secondhand pairs of pants and basketballs. Confront the Catholics of Omaha with the racism they were allowing and fostering.

Meanwhile Krejei and I tried to keep ourselves and the parish together, and people did start flocking to the services. It was a vicarious thing for a lot of them, I guess—we were getting our heads busted—but many were ready to witness. But the clergy . . . I spent a whole year after that without once being invited out to another parish for Forty Hours or Confirmations; those were just accepted things where pastors invited one another.

In June, when the new appointments were ready, the personnel board wanted to send me away to school in St. Louis. And they joked that St. Louis hadn't any civil-rights trouble and that it would be a nice place for me to rest up. I was ready to go at that point; I was still an obedient servant of the church. But the word filtered down that the reason I was being transferred was because I wasn't working with the pastor-builder of the basketball courts. I went back to the personnel board and confronted them with the fact that for a whole year, every Thursday from nine P.M. until three or four in the morning, we had meetings in the rectory toward bettering social conditions in this city and neighborhood, and that pastor never made one of them. Could it be possible he wasn't working with us? I told them I didn't play basketball so good any more and there were other things to do in this neighborhood. I told them no, I couldn't accept the reassignment.

I told them they could dump me out of the social action office, which they did, but if they took me out of Holy Family I'd picket the chancery office and I could get plenty of people to do it. They eased off on me, but they shipped John Krejei out to the Indian mission, literally—it's up in Winnebago. He spent a year there, a year at Notre Dame, after which he had just had it. He got married a year ago June. He probably left for the same reason that was going through my mind: the structure was not going to change. They still can control the lives of people who could possibly help change the situation in our city; we would never really be effective because they could pull the cork at any time.

And secondly, John must have felt—as I felt—under such pressure and without the warm, loving support of anybody. The normal male would just as soon get out and get that support from a loving female. That was the real problem, support. I used to drive out to the country and just sit in my car and cry. Not only because I was alone but because the people on top didn't understand, didn't care to understand, and weren't going to change. A few nuns were saying, "Right on," but that was it for support.

I tried to keep the chancery abreast of what we were doing, but they were getting thousands of letters saying things like Get McCaslin out, he's besmirching the name of the church. And they forwarded all those letters along to me. They filled a big toilet-paper box; they're still around here somewhere as a testimony to something. And this is where I reached the point of asking whether I could do the things that needed to be done outside the church—no, I could never leave the church—but outside the priesthood.

That was later in 1968 and I just broke down from pure exhaustion. Maybe it was the beginning of a nervous breakdown; I was physically and emotionally shot. I told few people I was in the hospital. For four days I just rested and thought and prayed. And the question kept coming up: Can I do it better outside the priesthood where no bishop, no personnel board can use me as their puppet? But then, I knew, I couldn't be a liturgist. I couldn't lead a community in worship. Most importantly, I wouldn't have the chances to get into people's lives.

My conclusion, when I cut that hospital band off my wrist after four days, was: By jingo, I am church too. I understand what the problems are and they don't, and somebody has to stay who can try to make other people understand, and they ain't getting me out of the church. Direct from the hospital I went to the bishop and I said, politely, "I'm not leaving the priesthood, I'm not leaving the church, I'm not leaving the Archdiocese of Omaha, and if you want to get me out of any one of these three you have to fire me."

He did none of the three.

So now I have a base at Holy Family Church to which people come because, first, they are interested in good worship and, second, because the message of the church in the establishment of brotherhood and justice and morals and peace means something to them. When I was a social activist I had little time to think. Now I have more time to be priest. My life after 1968 and 1969 and up to today centers on worship and building a Christian community of people from all over the city who go back into their neighborhoods and spread what we develop here. I have scars from my social activist days and they are slow in healing. The days of marches are over anyhow, because they almost always end in violence and I'm a nonviolent person.

I can think back to another event that helped me refocus my priesthood. It was after a day and a night of meetings, meetings, meetings, most of them useless, with a lot of ranting and raving. I just stopped my car between meetings and said, "McCaslin, this is insanity." So I slipped into the back of the church and spent the whole day thinking and praying and wishing and hoping and crying and praying some more. I lay down and took a nap. It was a hot August afternoon and the church was stuffy and I woke up drenched. My only conclusion was that a hundred years from now priests won't have to go through this particular form of agony. And I began to realize that I was a liturgist and I could build community and send people out and not have to run around like a crazy man. This isn't to say that social action wasn't justified. I just wanted to make sure that whatever I did was going to be based in the Eucharist, in the Christ, in Christian community, and not in McCaslin's ego trip or Savior complex.

It would be foolish to say I settled anything that day, the four days in the hospital, or that everything is straight in my head now. It isn't. My hands shake. I smoke too much and I have a lot of doubts. For instance, even for a comparatively old codger like me, celibacy remains a problem, although right now if the church said I could marry, I would not. I have loving relationships now with many people, three women-people, and I have the normal male hormones and cells, and to live the life of celibacy is very difficult at times. But I think I live it more comfortably now because of the developed relationship with Christ that has come about through an attempt at real prayer. I might even call myself a happy celibate —but not always a contented one. Actually, for my own contentment, I would still make a perpetual vow of celibacy today.

From the practical side of it I would be a bad husband, and if I had kids I would be a bad father. I think I can best do the work I believe Christ has called me to do by being celibate. I see an unending stream of dope addicts, alcoholics . . . Like the day before Christmas I spent four hours with a girl who had a gun to her head, trying to convince her to give the gun to me. I really wouldn't want to expose a wife and children to all that.

Celibacy is so overblown. That isn't the issue on priests' minds; it's our whole framework. I believe that Jesus set up a hierarchical structure—not what we have today with the Princes of the Church —but people who are at once in positions of authority but are foot washers and servants of the people, the chief listeners. I think about being a bishop; I make no bones about that. And I'd resign if I couldn't make it work. I want to see if the church really could be reformed from the top as well as from within.

Looking back over almost twenty years in the priesthood, there were two real crisis periods. In 1963 it was the new theology; in 1968 it was whether or not I could most effectively live out my life as a priest. In both of those crisis times Christ became the one I could depend on. I didn't know what I believed, but I believed in him and I was telling him, "You've got to find me a route that I've got to go. I'm not smart enough to figure it out on my own."

And both times I came out, not stronger necessarily, but with a different orientation. In 1968 especially I found I couldn't depend on the institution I was so enmeshed with for support. I couldn't depend on the community and companionship of my brother priests. I found that if I'm going to survive qua priest and qua Christian, I have to set about to intensify a life in Christ and build a faith community where peace and love and justice and brotherhood and not rubrics are the standards.

Funny, I really do believe that the kind of confusion right now can be the opportunity of turning the church around. Maybe parishes as we knew them are dead and they have to go. Something else will spring up. But I find myself more patient in the process now, and I have the feeling I'm not beating my head against an unbudgeable stone wall. Because every time the head gets bloodied the wall must give a bit. We just have to realize that a lot of heads are needed to be battering rams.

I feel "the times they are a-changin'." We used to get a letter a month from the archbishop reprimanding us about something going on down here. He doesn't write those letters any more. People who came back to church by coming here are back in their own parishes and are leading the praying and singing there. In that sense people are seeing a validity in what we have been doing here, what we have and will stand for. I see the change in the archbishop. He is beginning to listen. We have to take him where he's at, but he's listening more. And he can grow into a great archbishop someday.

Father Charles Tobin

The priest at the five-thirty P.M. *Mass at St. Mark's Church in Independence, Missouri, beckons to the dozen worshipers to gather around the altar as he begins the Offertory. As he goes through the ritual he makes eye contact with the participants, almost as if he were trying to talk to them about what was going on instead of merely reciting the required words.*

Father Charles Tobin, thirty-one, in full clerical garb, including a Roman collar, says a personal word to each person as they leave the church and then he walks slowly, almost reluctantly, toward the rectory. Two sets of objects in his room immediately catch the eye. Intertwined amidst the shelves on the wall in back of his bed is a riot of small Christmas lights, a delicate festival of colors winding in and out of books, art objects—and clocks. There are four alarm clocks. The first turns on the lights, the second an FM station with semi-classical music, and the third and fourth do the actual waking up. Chuck Tobin is very conscientious about not oversleeping, not giving anyone the chance to criticize him for being late.

His room in the rectory is allegedly a priest's retreat, his home, his place for relaxation, ease. But another object contradicts this. On the night stand there is a private telephone so he can receive calls after hours. His pastor (whom he addresses as "Father" and who in turn addresses him as "Father") and the pastor's mother, who also lives in the house, are in bed by ten. Chuck Tobin eats many of his meals at the local hamburger drive-ins just for a chance to get away. He turns up the radio to cover his conversation as he talks with friends. Paranoia? Perhaps, but Chuck Tobin has reason to know that he is not a man to be trusted, that he is suspect.

He came out of an Irish Catholic tradition in rural Missouri that has produced many priests who went on to long, peaceful clerical careers and who were eulogized as "other Christs." Why should Chuck Tobin have had all the trouble he did? After all, with a brother, Father Patrick Tobin, who was ordained by Bishop John Patrick Cody in St. Patrick's Church, and a mother who made great sacrifices after her husband died to send all her children to Catholic schools, why shouldn't this Tobin have had an easier go of it?

Some might say he was a little too independent. For instance, he didn't graduate from grade school and leap into a minor seminary. In fact he didn't enter until he had finished St. Benedict's College, where he took no theology courses and concentrated in sociology, psychology, and education. He was in drama, he made Who's Who in American Colleges, *he drove a combine for the wheat harvest in the plains states, he worked summers in Washington for the FBI and for the House Education and Labor Committee. All the while priesthood was at the back of his mind, but he kept delaying the step. He looked at the Benedictines, and at first was taken by their family-ness but later decided against them because they seemed too docile, too unquestioning.*

He finally put plans for graduate school aside and entered the diocesan priesthood. From the beginning, seminary enraged him. There were foolish rules, there were cassocks, there was—sin of all sins—wasted time.

His priesthood, because of his creative nature, took a different turn. Chuck Tobin was one of the "new" priests, fascinated by audio-visuals instead of catechisms, Marshall McLuhan, the latest book on practical psychology like I'm OK, You're OK. *He turned aside study in Rome to stay in the United States and keep his emphasis pastoral rather than theological. He involved himself heavily in religious education and found he could work well with young people. But paralleling his interest and efforts in the new forms of making the Gospel understandable to people of this generation came a series of events that formed the Chuck Tobin of today. Events that showed him the lack of sensitivity the church had toward the creative, the offbeat. Events that made a more cautious man out of what was essentially a free spirit.*

Misunderstanding.

Insensitivity.

I want to keep those two words in mind as I try to tell about myself. First of all, a confession: I'm a terrible rambler and a favorite phrase of mine is "to make a long story longer," so I'm going to try to center my story around a few events that might show the hurt that is inflicted unnecessarily into a priest's life. And maybe it is that kind of hurt or misunderstanding or insensitivity that has driven other men out of the priesthood. I could easily today be among their number.

Most of us can remember those pietistic teachings we used to get that priests would be saved automatically. I didn't go into the seminary until an older age, but as much as we all laugh about that kind of teaching today, it must have made its mark. After doing my student teaching I found myself questioning, searching, wondering: Did I have a vocation? I liked teaching, so why not go into that? I also was wondering if I wasn't just following my brother Pat into the priesthood and if the nice way of life priests had and the respect weren't the main factors. I could teach, I could go on in psychology, but the thoughts about priesthood were very strong.

For some people Conception Abbey was a paradise of a seminary; for me the four years there were four long, impatient years when I felt I was often treated like a child. By the time I got to Conception I had worked in all kinds of jobs, thanks to my brother Maurice, and had spent a lot of time with Pat in the rectory, so I didn't feel like a naïve kid. At the seminary I never felt challenged; it was more of a lock-step mentality. Okay, we have this impatient young man gritting his teeth through the seminary days, but still convinced of the priesthood. I believe strongly in the concept of call, and the priesthood was my call.

During the deacon year we were allowed to work in a parish on weekends and for the summer. Monsignor Baum, who is now the Archbishop of Washington, D.C., was over me, and he gave me a lot of support and understanding and listened to my frustrations. That year I ran into a series of friends I hadn't seen in years who made me question myself. Like Helen Sullivan. I hadn't seen her since high school. She had gone into religious life, worked with Father Bob Fox in Harlem, and had left. Here was a woman who had gone enthusiastically into religious education, had her ideas rejected wholesale, and was questioning values and becoming more and more radical in wanting to get back to her roots. She kept asking, Hey, aren't we in a post-Christian era? Christianity was fine as a culture, but . . . She was fascinated by the fact that I was going into the priesthood, and she wasn't shy about saying she thought it was rather dumb.

Helen was great. She asked me, "Hey, who's Jesus?"—things I'd never asked myself—and it really started me questioning. But it was liberating, it got me out of a seminary mentality and into a life context. I was aware of doubts as I approached ordination but I felt very strong about that sense of call.

Then came one of those times of insensitivity or inability to understand needs. The seminary cut us off from going out into parishes on weekends. Some guys had abused it—left on Thursday and came back on Monday morning and did little pastorally in between. I felt resentment at being herded, at being treated like a child. But I still went to my assigned parish and continued talking with people like one of the parishioners who was the editor of *Community Now,* which started after *The Catholic Reporter* folded. Helen would come out to the parish, and a whole bunch of us would rap on and on about the question: Is even Christianity valid, let alone the priesthood?

About March or April before ordination, with the invitations out and my head full of questions that our blah retreats at the seminary never confronted, I talked to Bill Baum late into one night. I told him I was scared to death. I was about to be ordained and I was still questioning who God is.

Bill was beautiful. He listened patiently and then he said, "Chuck, I hope that on your deathbed you're still trying to figure out what in the devil His relationship is to you." And that was tremendously reassuring, to know he had the same doubts I did; that a person could still say yes in the midst of all this wondering. Strangely enough, I couldn't share those doubts with my priest brother or other members of the family then. They were looking forward to my ordination with pride, and I didn't want to disappoint them.

I wanted to be ordained at the little rural church in my home town of Burlington, but it was so small and I wanted to share this with so many people that I arranged for the gymnasium at Mount Alverno Academy in Maryville. I felt it could be an educational event for them too, and so many of them were a part of my call in some way or another that I felt an obligation to them.

Also I was headstrong. I wanted the celebration of that day to be meaningful, symbolic, moving, dramatic, religious—everything in one day. A nun made a thirty-by-thirty-foot banner for the backdrop that took the words from Kennedy's inaugural address, "God's Work Must Truly Be Our Own," and those words were on the prayer cards. And that theme was going to be followed in the sermon by Father Ed Hayes the next day for my first Mass. Together we had worked it out where he would say that we were all doing God's work and that I was not that special.

I used the Jerusalem cross in the invitations and announcements, and on the huge banner there was an abstract version of it. It is the large cross with the four small crosses, and it had the bad connotation of being the Crusaders' Cross, but to me it's a mission cross, symbolizing the idea of us being sent to the four corners of the world.

Townspeople were wonderful. I asked a fellow who owned a carpet company if we could use some carpet in the altar area, and he went ahead and built a low platform so everyone could see the altar and then covered it with a lush red carpeting. In my church in Burlington they had a gorgeous big bold table for an altar and they brought it over gladly.

I had studied dramatics in college, taught it in high school, and I was very aware of the kinds of things that focused people's attention. I wanted to create an atmosphere of warmth, I wanted communion under both species, bread and wine, for everyone. And all this I cleared through Bill Baum, who was then chancellor. We had twenty chalices on the altar, banners all over the place, a procession arranged where a lot of relatives and kids would carry in more banners. The Knights of Columbus wanted to be a part of it, and they had their plumes and swords and everything.

Bishop Helmsing was going to officiate and I had asked him in private one day if it would be all right if the master of ceremonies could be a priest from Conception who would be relaxed with the little different things we were going to do. This day meant a lot to me, I had planned it for months, and the MC that the bishop usually had along with him was a brusque, blunt man who acted as though whatever he was doing was just a job to get done without regard for people's feelings.

The ordination was to take place at two, and at three minutes to two the bishop arrived. Of course we were frantic about where he was. I had set up a special room for the bishop to vest in so he could have a little time to himself, and I thought that would please him. My aunt Vivian, who was a seamstress, had made him beautiful white vestments with the Jerusalem cross on the front and back and some very fragile chain adorning them.

Shortly after the bishop arrived my brother Pat came to me and said, "Charles, now don't get excited, just keep calm. It's ordination day and we have to go through with things. He's brought his own MC along and he's changing everything out there. Now Charles, be calm."

There were probably a thousand people in the auditorium when the MC went to the altar. The PA system was on, so everyone heard "Get this stuff out of here." Twenty chalices filled with wine, beautiful candles—not just the traditional six—just shoved off the altar. Then he scooped up the fragile vestments, threw them in a chair in the principal's office, told the bishop he would vest in there, and locked the door.

He told the bishop this guy Tobin was trying to do a lot of stuff behind his back; he didn't get permission on both species, he didn't check on this, on that. And I had, through the chancellor. The next thing I knew this MC was standing in front of me. "His Excellency would like to see you immediately." Oh, yeah? Oh, God, why today?

I guess this was symbolic of the troubles that would follow. Here was a day that could have been made very special. The bishop talked to me like a child, saying that I hadn't gotten permission, and his voice said he was very angry with me. "I have a mind not to let anybody receive under both species."

Just the week before, the bishop had given a talk at a priest's jubilee, a beautiful, theologically great talk about the priesthood, and I was so happy he was going to talk at the ordination and hoped he would explain to the people the whole concept of what was going on in the church and with the priesthood. Instead his talk centered around the importance of priests being obedient to their bishops and the need to suffer in the church today. It just wasn't the same bishop I had heard the week before. People were hurt, crushed, that day. I among them.

The next day the first Mass went well and Ed did a great job of mending some fences with his homily. I was all right by then. I have an ability to bounce back or I wouldn't be here. For the next four months I was assigned to my home parish, and it was four months of saying thank you to wonderful people, many of whom I'd known since I was a kid. My message was simple: "You've got ability, worth, and you'll want to do something with all that."

I was assigned to a parish in Lee's Summit, an older suburban area of Kansas City, to work there on a half-time basis and half-time at a girls' high school, St. Theresa's Academy. Later some work on the diocesan marriage tribunal was thrown in. It was frustrating from the start because I never had enough time for any job. At the parish I found I was good with the young, which I didn't think I would be. We started doing audio-visual things, creating some of our materials, doing multi-projector happenings. We put together *Born Free,* which was about freedom and world peace, using songs like "Abraham, Martin, and John," "Impossible Dream," and "Exodus," and it was shown in many parts of the United States. The end product wasn't as important as the chance to put it together and let the kids express themselves.

The kids started tutoring in the inner city. There were street cleanup things, and the Black Panthers jumped all over us for our paternalism. But that was good for our suburban kids to face; they learned volumes about race relations in a few months. And so did I.

I thought it would be good for the girls at mostly white St. Theresa's to have the opportunity to hear what the blacks were going through. So I set up an assembly for the juniors and seniors to hear

Lee Bohannan, who was active in the black movement. He talked for a couple minutes, then asked for questions. One of the girls asked about his views on interracial marriage. And Lee said something off the cuff like "Is that a request for a date?" or something. The girl was extremely embarrassed, but I didn't think much about it and we went on.

The assembly was at noon and I didn't get back to the rectory until after four. We had an elderly housekeeper all alone there who had been suddenly besieged with calls like "Is that nigger-loving son of a bitch Tobin there?" She was in a panic when I got there. The calls kept coming in, and they were raw. At school the next day we were called together for a seven o'clock conference on what was to be done; the principal had gotten her share of calls too. I thought, here it is: get-Tobin day. To my surprise, tremendous surprise, they weren't out to get me. The principal wanted me to apologize to the girls. Most of the rest of the faculty felt it was the parents, not the school or Chuck Tobin, who needed to apologize.

I had had some pretty enlightening calls from parents, and I wanted to share them with the juniors and seniors, so we had an assembly. The PA system was turned up loud, but I spoke softly and said, "I walked in there thinking I should apologize to you, but after the calls I got from your parents last night I've decided I really don't owe you an apology. After I realized how little Christianity there is in some of your parents, I can understand and excuse and just forget any misunderstanding that you might have had." I told them about all the profanity; the parents calling me a long-haired (I wasn't) liberal priest, telling me I was trying to get their daughters pregnant by a black man. And I described a seventy-year-old housekeeper who didn't know what had happened. It took me about four minutes, and half the kids were in tears. We had twenty-six minutes left, and I suggested maybe we should talk about this whole racial thing a bit more. They began talking to one another, not really to me. I ended by saying I'd be in the rectory by two and I'd take calls as late as people wanted to talk.

At six-thirty the next morning I got finished with the last call. Mostly it was just letting people talk out their anger, and I think that reached a lot of people and made them rethink some of the stereotyped clichés they were tossing around. One guy missed the point and said if I wanted blacks to speak he could get some of the "boys" from his shop.

My work at the marriage tribunal was routine and a drag—going through papers, double-checking evidence, and writing up cases to be sent to Rome—work that any secretary could have done. That part of my ministry I hated. I still was very sure of my call, sure that part of my call was to upset people, confront them, and I felt good about that.

But I was torn three ways and I found myself wanting to concentrate more and more on religious education, using audio-visual and multimedia stuff. I knew it was the way to reach kids, but there was no money and almost no time. I didn't take days off, I stayed broke paying for stuff out of my own pocket, even having trouble with my car payments.

Father Larry Graham had built up a beautiful diocesan religious education program and he asked if I wanted to come work in his office full time. It was at a time when the reaction to Larry was at its highest pitch. Conservative pastors were calling for his head. He knew his funding was going to be cut way back. He and Father Pete Cole were going to try to keep the thing going. There were rumors around that Larry was leaving the priesthood, but rumors were always flying. When I left St. Theresa's the rumor was that I was leaving too. They even picked the nun I was running off with. Well, Larry did leave, and so did Pete. Which left me moving to cramped quarters with only two people in the office. I was angry because I thought I knew Larry and Pete, and neither gave me an idea he was going.

I found out where the paper clips were and what desk I could use and I set up shop. I visited a lot of priests to find out what we should be doing. They wanted nice, safe religious-education stuff in the great volume that the office had provided over the past years with its huge staff. That overwhelmed and depressed me.

Maybe for the first time I started questioning. What was I really doing? I really hadn't been a success at St. Theresa's, really never got the chance to work in depth with people at Lee's Summit, and I was disappointed at the tribunal office. I'd been a priest for two years and this was my fifth job. I didn't have any roots, didn't have any friends I could relate to, because I was always jumping around. But I really jumped into the religious ed job, pushed the people I worked with, started going to some conferences. And the same story kept coming up about people in religious ed eventually leaving the religious life because when they grasped the Christian message they found the church at large didn't want to hear it.

I couldn't stand good old Kavanaugh for a long time, but he came out with his book* saying that there are men too gentle to live among wolves, that you could only take insensitivity so long. But for me the doubts about priesthood were still faint and certainly not as pained as they would be later. I could still put up with the institution.

Therese Fitzgerald, with her process orientation, worked with me and really taught me wonders. About how you bring people alive to see things as their own responsibility instead of preaching to them through our materials. At first it was hard to see that we could do anything. I was down a lot in those early months.

To give us some orientation we set up a three-day workshop early in February. Father Jack Russell, who was head of the national office of Directors of Religious Education, gave us the latest trends and a vision of where we ought to be going. The bishop was there, college people, retreat people, everybody in adult Christian education. But I still wasn't that confident we could implement whatever plans might develop, get people moving. Was the hassle, was the negative feedback all worth it? Jack took me aside near the end of the workshop—and I'll never forget this—and just sat me down

* *A Modern Priest Looks at His Outdated Church.*

and said that a lot of people were getting hassled and had doubts whether or not they were accomplishing anything. And then he said a beautiful thing: "Hey, have you kind of forgotten that Jesus is with you?" And from that meeting, so rich in new visions and plans and all, Jack's words are what I really remember.

We did show Jack our plans for the next year and he liked them, and when he left town it signaled a turning point. During February I got two great nuns to be staff members. They had fantastic backgrounds and were a bit older, but very with it. Things were building up and, in the terminology of transactional analysis, we were getting positive strokes, better feedback.

We were looking forward to Father Ed Hayes's "Electronic Benediction" on February 28. Because he had given my first Mass sermon, things seemed to be coming full circle. Ed used a strobe light playing on a cross, causing it to shimmer as he took the huge audience through history and showed how people had seen the crucifixion, painted it, or rendered it. Granted there wasn't any host as in the traditional benediction, but it really was a way of glorifying the Father through Christ and calling people to an awareness of suffering and the purpose of the cross.

Therese and I had invited a few people to get together afterwards and we were elated, talking about the benediction, the plans for the next year. There were maybe a half-dozen religious. One of them was Sister John Bosco, who was very talented and deeply involved in religious education. I had known her for a month, and I got to know a little about her and her enthusiasm for the new things she wanted to do. And I felt close to her because I found out she had had Hodgkin's disease and she had at one time been sent back to her mother house, knowing she was going to die. The month she was supposed to die they tried some experimental drug on her, and it did arrest it. She had been through hell and had been put in the infirmary with other sisters who were very sick, even psychologically; one had committed suicide.

Anyway, the gathering didn't last long, and when I got to my car

I found a role-playing game called "Cans of Squirms" that Sister John Bosco had lent me. I went to her car to return it, and she had some questions about some of the new materials. So we just sat in the car for a few minutes and talked about the stuff, never thinking about locking the doors or anything. This was in a good area of Kansas City, Missouri, right off the Plaza, which is theoretically the city's pride.

Suddenly there were these two guys, one at each door, and before I knew it they shoved their way into the front seat and the first thing I remember was a gun stuck in my face. One of them took off my glasses right away, but I still could see him clearly. He wasn't harsh, but cocky, and acted like he was on a high. Okay, Tobin, I said, be able to identify him, keep cool about how you're going to try to disarm him and let Sister get free. The guy on the driver's side started to pull away from the curb and the other guy removed my watch and asked how much money we had. Sister was very cooperative. She said she would give them all she had, something like six dollars. I was a lot more reluctant. When he reached into my coat pocket I tensed up.

"Ah hah," he said, "we've got something here." It was my appointment book, but it felt like a wallet.

As we drove off I began to put two and two together. We were in a residential area on a narrow street, and if they got us out in the country we wouldn't have a way of defending ourselves. And all I could see was death. I could see them not finding enough money on us and killing us alongside some quiet country road.

I figured if I could somehow have him crash into a parked car that would cause attention, anything. I guess I was bold enough with the police work I had done in Washington that I figured I could go for his gun. So I relaxed and he went after my appointment book, meanwhile turning the gun to the side. I went for it and held it away from us, but the other guy also had a gun and he started pistol-whipping me over the head. Somehow I reached across with my foot and jammed it in the horn ring, which at least made them stop long enough for the guy on the driver's side to get my foot out. Meanwhile he was still beating me with the gun and the blood was coming down and I couldn't see very well and I knew I was losing consciousness.

The horn, our screaming, this car crazily parked in the middle of the street—nothing caused anybody to come out and see what was going on. Then I think two of their buddies joined them and pulled me out of the car and really started beating me, throwing me against the side of the car. Finally I slumped to the ground, just about unconscious, and I remember one of the guys pulling out his gun, aiming it at me, and firing. I didn't know where it hit. I wondered if I was dying.

I was on the ground in front of the car and I saw the headlights coming toward me and that's the last thing I remember. Evidently they swerved around me. A couple on the street—oddly enough a black couple in this white neighborhood—had called the police and they were there within seconds, I guess, but two of the guys with Sister were already gone. All the police could see was this beaten, bloody man in the middle of the street; they couldn't know what else had happened.

It wasn't until a half-hour later that I regained partial consciousness to tell them what had happened. Meanwhile, the two guys took Sister to an inner-city area and raped her. She was in such a weakened condition from Hodgkin's disease that she couldn't put up much resistance. Finally when they were through they asked her if she knew how to get home and she said, "I live in a convent; I'm a Catholic nun." They didn't know what that was, but it scared them. One of the guys found a rosary on Sister and said he wanted it. And she gave it to him. They were concerned that she get back home, so they drove to a main street, got out, and disappeared.

The reports of the incident broke about seven A.M. and the bishop was at the hospital soon after. I was drowsy and couldn't talk much and he didn't say much either. He took hold of my hand in both of his and just held it. That said volumes to me of warmth, support, all kinds of things. Nothing about Chuck, what were you doing out with a nun at that hour of the morning? and no trite *fervorinos*. I really feel the Holy Spirit was with him that day, because if he had in any way come down on me I doubt I'd be here today.

The news reports started off with "A priest and nun sitting in a parked car were accosted." They kept adding little things like "He was dressed in his clericals, the sister was not." So by that evening it was a banner headline—"Priest Beaten, Robbed; Nun Raped"—and the story about the parked car, me in black, Sister in street clothes. There had been a lot of stuff about priests and nuns leaving, so people could read a lot into it, and the papers and stations played it up big and were really titillating the public. It was on national news broadcasts that night. The local papers kept the story going day in and day out as a suspect was released or one of my credit cards was found. Anything to dredge up the whole business.

My family responded beautifully and were quickly at my side. People by the jillions rallied to my support. I was not allowed any visitors, but the phone switchboard was lit up and cards poured in. Sister John Bosco, on the floor above me, sat alone except when my friends would go up to see her. Her bishop never came, never called. None of the sisters from the convent came. Finally two sisters from the mother house paid a token visit. She didn't have the chance for support that I did, because my name was in the papers and hers wasn't. And she had the reputation of being a very open person, not the traditional nun who would wear the right clothes, be at the right place, and be back at the right time. Some must have felt she deserved what she got.

Then one nun called her and said how sad it was what her bishop had done. "My bishop?" she asked. The bishop, I assume, because of the stickiness and the scandal and all, said that she couldn't return to her convent or his diocese—ever.

She had no way of verifying this until a call came through later from the bishop. He said he hoped she was getting better and that he'd be glad to do all he could to help her relocate. There were no choices; the outcast was to go.

Not long after, the police picked up a guy who tried to cash a $300 check at Sears using one of my credit cards. He said he got it from another guy, who was one of the line of men they brought into the hospital auditorium for possible identification, handcuffed to one another. It was so depersonalizing and ugly. The night of the incident I had bitten the wrist of the guy I was struggling with. One of the fellows in the lineup looked like him and I said to the detective, "Look at the right wrists of all those men and see if any have scars from recent teeth marks." One did. The one I recognized.

That wasn't much consolation during those days in the hospital. When the news broadcasts had finally calmed down they let me have a radio. Simon and Garfunkel had a new song out that just seemed to fit the moment. The lines "When you're down and out, when you're on the street" were for me. And the last part, about "Sail on, silver girl," seemed to be for Sister John Bosco.

I wanted to see the bishop very badly, to make it clear that we were just talking in the car. I was starting to get feedback. One doctor said, "Now, Father, you're going to have to face this like a man, move to another diocese, and continue your work." I was naïve about the whole thing until the word started filtering down from on high that something was going to have to be done with Tobin, that he had caused scandal to the priesthood.

I knew Sister John Bosco was going to be exiled, a sick woman who had been mercilessly raped. I knew something was in store for me, who had gotten my head pulverized and leg shot, when I got on a plane for Washington. I went to my brother Maurice's apartment and spent about three weeks there resting and thinking.

I faced myself with the fact that I was becoming a more warm and open person, that I wanted to love people, not like them at an acceptable clerical distance. I knew I would go back a marked man.

Whenever I would be seen alone with a nun or a woman, I knew wheels would be spinning in people's minds.

My brother Pat and I had talked before about things priests should and shouldn't do. He had felt a priest shouldn't be out of blacks, even at family reunions. A priest was celibate and celibacy meant no deep relationships with people. He should find his company only with other priests. All that was totally against my nature.

My last week in Washington was Holy Week and I did a lot of thinking, reading, and praying. It came to me slowly the kind of priest I would have to be if I stayed. I wouldn't feel compelled to wear clericals just to show I was really a priest. I would take risks, love, be hurt, get close, take discouragements, not be bitter, not be blind to the fact that I was a person who was changing every day.

My decision came on Holy Saturday, just as I was ready to go back home. I wanted to be there on Easter because the announcement of Bill Baum as bishop was going to be made. Holy Saturday, symbolism all over the place. I had decided I'd live day by day, but that I'd make a new commitment each Holy Week and never be naïve enough to say, Yea, sure, I'm going to be a priest forever, in the sense of never having any openness to what the future might hold. But I did want to say a simple yes to God's call to suffering and new life. So I came back resurrected. I knew it wouldn't be easy, but I was going to make it as myself.

In my meeting with the bishop I expected that I would take the lead, explain myself, tell him how positively I felt about the priesthood and that I wanted to get going again. But as soon as I sat down in his office he took the lead and I just listened. The event had embarrassed him. He was getting feedback from other bishops. "Oh, what's going on with those young priests and nuns in Kansas City anyhow?" I had caused a scandal. The diocese didn't need this kind of thing. The whole tone was punitive and it brought back memories of ordination day. He was not pleased with me; the errant son had offended the father.

During that meeting with the bishop the phrase "We have to be realistic" kept coming up. Then finally the blow. I was being replaced immediately in the religious education job. The guy who was to replace me was at the other pole from the things we were trying to introduce. I was laid low, but that decision I'd made on Holy Saturday was not "Yes, if," it was "Yes, damn it!" And whatever work they tell me to do I'm going to give it my best.

The pastor at St. Mark's had asked for me specifically because he wanted somebody to work with young people, and I purposely forced myself to look forward. I knew there were two older, alive nuns in their religious education center. I knew there was a contemporary Mass group already formed and they could become a good support group. I'm a person who needs support desperately; I need to care about people and have them care about me. At first when I arrived I couldn't quite get the thing in balance, and there was a need to create new friendships.

Coming from the religious ed scene to a parish where I really didn't know people and had to be careful, I began to feel the pain and hesitancy of creating new relationships in the vacuum left by the sudden change. It was as if I had been in front of a warm fire and then stepped out into the cold weather and could feel it ten times more than if I'd been in the barn and walked out from there. I had come from the warmth of people who gathered around me after the incident to the routine of parish life.

At first the pastor talked about splitting the parish and for me to be responsible for my half. Then I began to have some beautiful unstructured home liturgies, and things were beginning to jell. The kids were awakening, working on audio-visual projects at the church till all hours and doing lots of searching during retreats and home religion sessions. Then I began to sense that the pastor wasn't all that approving of where I was going. I think he wanted me to visit homes all day—and I did a lot of that.

Finally he said I was working with the youth too much. So I cut back some on that. I tend to want to please people, and if that would please the pastor I would do it. In the rectory, I didn't always feel at home, and ever so often we failed to communicate over issues of liturgy, clerical dress, or content of teaching. Although we both recognized the differences I knew that I at least did not have the talent, courage, or the charity to really overcome the lack of communication. Henri Nouwen has a book called *Intimacy* that has really spoken to me. He says that there is often so little communication in a rectory that a young priest spends all his time outside with a few couples because he gets good feedback from them and then isolates himself from his work. I tried very hard not to do that, but I had gotten close to a few couples, and without them I wasn't sure how I could survive.

After the first year at St. Mark's I was able to make my Holy Week commitment for another year in the priesthood, but there was a lot of sorrow in my heart. During that year Sister John Bosco had spent six rough months at her mother house. She's a person who wants to share things and they made it such a hush-hush thing that she felt like an outcast. Talk about insensitivity and lack of support, she really experienced both. I knew that Sister had grown close to a priest with whom she was working and the writing was on the wall. When it was finally announced that they were going to marry, I was proud to concelebrate their wedding Mass with her brother.

Before that Holy Week I had gotten to know a person I could be happy with, whom I could love. Things like that happen and you become so close to a person who shares your dreams, your thoughts, your frustrations that you find yourself one day facing what married priests and nuns have faced. I think we're all a little naïve about the mystery of love and really nurture relationships without knowing what they might involve. But that Holy Week a year ago I went through it all and said yes again to the priesthood.

Priesthood has become more and more people-oriented for me,

and as the summers were kind of slow here anyhow I asked the bishop if I could take one of Carl Rogers's courses in counseling out in La Jolla. The bishop said he had heard about places like that from a woman psychologist and that to go would have been putting myself in an occasion of approximate sin. That kind of response didn't blow my mind as it might have a couple years ago. It just made me sad and made me realize I was a bit more calloused and I wasn't going to let those things hurt me any more.

In the parish I was happy. With such a creative, dedicated, and fun religious and lay staff I saw the possibility of calling people to their potential. And did they ever have potential! So much talent, generosity, and leadership ability in such a young and new parish. Yet creativity was often unappreciated and efforts to participate more deeply in parish decisions and obtain wider personal involvement were frustrated. Parish council after parish council gave up. And yet good things continued to happen despite disappointments.

From time to time a gnawing concern over my commitment to Jesus came to the surface and I wondered if my yes to him was getting smothered in comfortable white Middle America. I really wasn't a great witness to the Lord in the way some men are: standing up against war, racism, or poverty. I lived in luxury, I wanted for nothing, I was spoiled. I wanted to follow him more radically, but my life style kept getting in the way. I had the chance to change apostolates and become involved in Newman work on campuses, but I chose to remain in my parish because I could still see the possibilities for growth there, the screaming needs of people to be cared for, loved, told they were worth something.

Misunderstanding, failures in communication, and the always present dull ache of loneliness continued. Yet the recent book *The Wounded Healer* has helped a little to transform those wounds into a positive force. I especially like the book's portrayal of the legend from the Talmud of the Messiah sitting among the poor, who are binding all their wounds at once. But he carefully binds his one at a time in order to be ready should he be needed to heal another. I found the book's suggestion that the priest's own wounds can be a source of healing for others to be realistic and helpful.

Another summer arrived. Two vacancies on our diocesan mission team in Bolivia had been open several months. My classmate John Seck had asked and received permission to go. When I congratulated him he jokingly invited me to join him. Two months later I said yes to Bolivia. And so on a summer day after my brother's wedding I announced to my family and close friends that I was going.

In a traditional departure ceremony the bishop usually presented a mission cross. People of the parish designed and made a simple wooden cross with the "being sent forth" Jerusalem symbol used on my ordination vestments. The bishop, before the ceremony, noting the lack of a corpus, expressed his hope that I not forget to meditate on the suffering Saviour. I remained silent but knew that the Messiah as "wounded healer" would never be far from my thoughts.

The separation from the youth, parish groups, family, and close friends was of course painful, knowing there would be some whom I would never see again. Yet, as flight 492 lifted high over Kansas City and all too quickly began to circle over La Paz, I knew that there would be a *someday*, a someday when I would be back for good. Meanwhile, another search had begun for the presence of the Messiah sitting at the gates of the city among the poor.

I cannot rationally put down why I stay a priest. In a recent letter from a student nurse of the parish, she asked what celibacy meant to me. I couldn't give a neat response. I could only explain that it was wrapped up in the yes to His beautiful and painful call.

Looking at people in the lay world has helped me stay in. Bob and Mary Kempen were an active couple in the parish, and then Western Electric transferred him to New Jersey. When we talked about Bob's work, which was essentially sensitivity training, getting people to loosen up, he talked about the frustrations, the amount of red tape that I'll never have to contend with in the church. And yet this guy keeps plugging away, seeing hope in little events, trying to bring a massive institution around.

Even in talking to guys who have left the priesthood I've found that if they had trouble with this institution they often have it with the other ones they have to work within. And marriage, as beautiful as it is, doesn't solve problems, it's not the panacea some men expected it to be.

I know I'm hurting a lot, my wounds aren't healed, but I also know I'd be hurting outside the priesthood. Just a few months ago I visited with Jack Russell, who eventually married Therese Fitzgerald, and I saw their beautiful baby and it was really good to be with them. Yet I wasn't really threatened. I didn't come away as I might have a year ago, saying, Gosh, I wish I were . . .

Father Richard Martin

Richard Martin would be fine material for Mr. Ripley and his journal of impossible people and events. The entry might go something like this: Richard Martin, born of a Unitarian mother and a staunch Irish Catholic father, was kicked out of one seminary and eventually attended three others before finally being ordained to the Roman Catholic priesthood. He then served briefly in a Virginia parish before taking a leave of absence, and—after four years in the world of women, flowered ties, and apartments—he has requested a return to the active ministry. Believe it or not!

Born and raised in strongly Catholic Providence, Rhode Island, Dick Martin was a product of an unconventionally religious home. His mother had such an aversion to priests as a young girl that she would cross the street when she saw one coming toward her. When her three children were ready for grade school, she adamantly proclaimed it would not be Catholic. Yet she made sure they attended catechism classes twice a week and attended church on Sundays and holy days of obligation.

She loosened up a bit as Dick reached high school age and allowed him to attend the Catholic boys' academy. Six months into his first year there, Dick shocked his mother by telling her he wanted to be a priest. Her response at first was silence, then she marshaled arguments why he shouldn't go. She had always been in the first pew when he served Mass and in the future she would be in the first pew as he participated as a deacon, then a priest, but Dick's mother was not initially inclined to see her first-born become a priest.

An outsider might have seen the signs. He was a quiet boy, more studious than his brother and sister. It was hard for him to make friends, but when he did make a good friend, the two of them would attend Tuesday night novenas together or stop into a church to say the Rosary. On the school bus in the morning, while the other kids jabbered away, Dick Martin would sit quietly, his right hand in his pocket, fingering a miniature rosary.

During his teenage years he became less of an introvert and attended dances. But he was the boy who would leave the crowd early to make sure he could get home before midnight to gulp down a glass of milk and a sandwich so he wouldn't violate his pre-Communion fast. Going to Communion each Sunday was a necessary part of Dick Martin's life.

At the seminary, after night prayers, three-quarters of the young men, including Dick, would dash around the huge cathedral visiting perhaps twenty of the side altars, saying special prayers to special saints. But, Dick Martin's religiosity and his never-ceasing desire to be a priest were not enough. He failed two subjects and committed an even more grievous sin: He had a "particular friendship" with two other seminarians. After three years he was told he had to leave, and the odyssey began that would take him through poor seminary and plush, from New England to the Deep South, that would finally culminate with his being ordained a priest.

The priesthood had its rewards for Dick Martin. It told him that he had worth. He enjoyed being with and serving people. Then the document that drove so many priests from the church almost took Dick Martin along in the tide. He read Humanae Vitae *and could not subscribe to its dogmatic stance against birth control.*

When he could no longer take what the priesthood in his Richmond parish had proved to be, he requested a leave of absence. Now in the fourth year of that leave of absence, he occupies a small office in Washington, D.C., working with drug addicts during the day, but saying Mass each morning and teaching religious education classes or doing volunteer counseling at night. As he talks in his office, a drug addict who is a transvestite comes in complaining of a toothache that has kept him from the typing classes that are part of his rehabilitation program. Dick Martin makes a dentist appointment for him that afternoon, gives him bus tokens and some soft, kind words.

He has enjoyed his people-oriented work for the last four years, but something has been nagging him. Now thirty-two, Dick Martin wants to go back into the active ministry.

For me it was never a sense of being called to the priesthood. It was more something that I thought I should try—try the seminary—and see if it was for me. I always loved that picture of a guy kneeling and Jesus Christ behind him with his hand on his shoulder, saying, "Come, follow me." I wanted that, but it never happened.

I wasn't the greatest scholastic at the seminary in Warwick, an average student—but when you're in a class of only twenty and you rank fifteenth or sixteenth! I did reasonably well in most subjects and basically I liked the seminary; I felt I wanted to go on, I wanted to be a priest. We had to put up with all the petty things that were typical of seminaries in those days. Your mail was censored, so we'd sneak out to the regular mailbox that was fifty feet from the dormitory, figuring our words were safer in the hands of Uncle Sam. The first page of the Providence *Journal* was tacked to the bulletin board; that was the extent of our news for the day.

Only those articles deemed most important by the faculty had the continuations tacked nearby. We were to be "in the world and not of it." We had to get special permission to listen to any kind of music that wasn't classical. The "1812 Overture" was popular; it was the loudest and most swinging music allowable.

Our home visits were limited and our parents couldn't come to see us except on special days, although my parents lived only five miles from the seminary. So seminarians figured ways around that. On a certain day each week we'd leave our laundry boxes in a room for our parents to pick up and do. A good friend, now ordained, Charlie Gilroy and I would sneak to the laundry room by an inside passageway during the fifteen-minute recreation period we had in the evening and get a visit with our families. I often thought how foolish all this must seem to my Protestant mother, but she always went along with our secret "visit."

Ten years ago there wasn't any turmoil on the campuses; ten years ago people did pretty much what they were told. We might have skirted the rules a bit but we never confronted the rules as unnecessary or unjust. Priests and nuns weren't leaving then. Our whole idea was that there were certain crosses to bear in life, and for the seminarian his cross was the rule book.

We were amazingly obedient. For instance, whenever a seminarian left or was asked to leave, they always made him go at a very discreet moment. You would go to lunch and come out, and your best friend could be gone. The guy who was leaving knew it, but he was told not to tell anyone, and they never did. Or you'd see a guy at lunch, be talking to him, and then you'd both head for prayer hall. He'd go down the corridor and in that half-hour he was packed and gone.

It was on the morning we were leaving for summer vacation in 1961 at the end of the third year that the rector said he wanted to see me at seven-thirty that night. A handful of guys were told to stay on and we all knew it wasn't because the rector wanted to give us medals of commendation. I walked into his office and he quite simply told me I didn't have a vocation for the diocese of Providence. I had flunked geometry and chemistry and on top of that myself and these two other fellows—they called us the Three Musketeers—were involved in a particular friendship. Anathema! If you walked with the same guy more than twice in one week you were particular friends. It was unrealistic, but we were supposed to become friends of the entire student body. The truth, however, was that in being with a different seminarian for nightly recreational walks you never developed a close friendship with anyone. Nowadays they encourage close intimate relationships.

The rector finished telling me why I didn't have a vocation and I told him in return that I was going on and I was going to become a priest. He said to me, "I hope you're not going on just for spite." No, I couldn't go on for spite. I just felt like the guy Sancho in *Don Quixote* when they asked him, Why do you follow this nut? And Sancho's only answer was I like him. My only answer was that I loved the priesthood.

It was the middle of June, rather late to be applying for a seminary opening in September. But I found the Holy Apostles Seminary in Connecticut, which is for men with delayed vocations. I went there and talked to the rector. They were just beginning their seminary. They needed men and I was accepted.

From a very wealthy seminary where they treated us like babies I went to a poor seminary where the average age was about forty. They were so poor they would go out in the evenings to the A&P and other stores to get leftover bread and leftover pastries. So poor that we had powdered eggs—and that was only on special occasions—and we drank our powdered milk out of wooden mugs. All the dishes were washed by hand. It was a primitive place; no heat in the buildings.

With older men like that they couldn't make the same demands they made on eighteen-year-olds, so we were more or less on our own and I responded well to that. During that year the vocation director from Richmond came hunting for men to come and finish their studies and work in his area, which was growing very fast and hurting for vocations. Other vocation directors approached us during the year, but being more impressed with Richmond, I eagerly accepted.

I did my major seminary work at St. Bernard's College in Alabama and to a Rhode Islander, Alabama is like Siberia. I remember ranting and raving to my mother, saying I didn't want to go there and I wouldn't go there. And she said, "Well, don't go." And I said, "But I have to."

I wanted this thing called priesthood; I didn't want the accidentals. But St. Bernard's turned out to be a tremendous experience. It was a very old, very poor seminary, run by the Benedictines, complete with farmlands and dairy—a beautiful pastoral setting. And it was relaxed; being farther down South certainly was better in many respects. My first seminary and last were lush, the two in the middle poor; and I really must say the spirit of the middle two was much, much better, more wholesome, more conducive to producing priests.

The theology department closed down in 1964 as vocations were beginning to slip, and all of us were sent to St. Francis Seminary in Loretto, Pennsylvania. This was the ultimate in seminaries. We called it antiseptically clean. Beautiful rooms, carpets, snack bars, the best equipment.

But an ironical thing happened at St. Francis. Every corridor of fifty guys had a deacon prefect, and I was named one of the deacon prefects. From being kicked out of the first seminary, I had gotten one of the highest positions available in the last seminary. I was supposed to enforce all these stupid rules that we still had. For instance, when I started seminary you could never go in another guy's room. At St. Francis the rule then was that you could be in the room providing part of you was outside the room. You could put a chair in the doorway and talk to the guy inside as long as half the chair was outside.

St. Francis was a seminary of philosophy and theology students, and yet, even at the age of postgraduate work, nobody was supposed to have a radio. I had one and so did a lot of people, and we just kept them out of view. I kept mine in a desk drawer and I had a set of ear plugs. When somebody knocked on the door, I slipped the whole business away. I just couldn't be strict about rules I didn't feel I could live by myself. Everyone had his own way of hiding a radio—from cigar boxes to fake books.

Four seminaries and nine years later I was ready for ordination. I chose an inscription for my patten that I still believe in very, very much today, something that sums up the whole idea of vocation: "I am the Good Shepherd." If you're not going to be a shepherd, get out of the whole thing. That's a little dramatic, but I felt that way in 1966 and I feel it today. I was hoping to lead people and I knew I wasn't going to do it solely by preaching from the pulpit. I think the greatest sermons are when the priest goes with the kids to the beach or on the football field, and that is where I gave some of my best sermons.

I feel personalism is one of the most essential ingredients in our sermons and especially in our Eucharists if they are to have any real meaning to our people. You're almost like a host at a party. If our parishioners get bored with the Mass, perhaps part of the difficulty lies with the routineness and impersonalism of the priest. If I'm in a church for the first time I'll say, "Good morning, I'm Dick Martin. I'm from the diocese of Richmond and I work with drug addicts in Washington." Eucharist is supposed to be a happy, friendly occasion.

When I did reach ordination I really felt that I had reached the most important goal of my life and that Jesus Christ must really want me. After going through all this hell there must be something that I was going to give, because I believed that God had a reason.

To get knocked down so many times and still get up and still have the same zeal at the end. Without being too proud, I really felt I was a chosen one. I saw in many of my classmates who never had a problem in their lives that they just zipped through all the years. I somehow felt a step ahead of them.

We had put a lot of emphasis on community in the last years in the seminary, and I could see communal strength as something that would support me in my work. The Benedictines always made it a point not only to teach us about community but to put their lessons into action. At mealtimes they sat with us, and when we had a movie they would mix right in among us. I came out thinking rectories were pretty much the same. I guess I was naïve enough to think that priests actually were automatically very charitable and kind and that there was a fraternal community in every rectory. There's a course now in some seminaries called pastor-assistant relations. I've heard it's a much more realistic view of what to expect. So many of us thought every rectory was one big happy community.

Anyway, I got my assignment and I was happy, elated it was in northern Virginia. It was a great parish, six thousand people, a good percentage of them in high-rises, mostly young and vibrant people. After three weeks' vacation we were supposed to report in time to hear confessions on a Saturday afternoon. So the young zealous curate arrived with bags, knocked on the door, and was met by the housekeeper. No welcoming party. Too bad it isn't a special occasion when somebody arrives at a rectory rather than when he leaves. He needs it when he gets there. The housekeeper called the pastor down and he said, "You're probably tired now. Rest up and you can hear confessions tonight." And that was about it.

I expected that when I said I was the new priest they would be sort of thrilled about it. I guess the housekeeper was more enthused about the new priest than the priests were. It dawned on me pretty quickly that the fraternal community wasn't exactly there, so I put that aside for a while and looked out to see where the flock was that this shepherd was going to tend. What I could see was a big recreation field in the back of the rectory, so I went to the kids. I wasn't the greatest baseball player, but when they were out there I was. I wasn't just their priest in the church, I was out there in my own clothes, being with them. The little ones would crawl all over me, but I thought this was one real way this group could identify with me. I can remember the kids best of all from those years. I'd get on a bus to go out to a beach party and they'd say, Wow, look at Father Martin; look at the clothes he's got. They all expected me to go around in black pants and a white T-shirt.

The first summer was a honeymoon and I loved parish work. The pastor was a great old man who for the most part let you learn by your own experience rather than warn and correct you all the time. He was such a good man that a lot of newly ordained priests who were having problems were sent to him by the bishop. The pastor felt I'd learn by my mistakes, but when I didn't think they were mistakes and he did that's where we'd have our problems.

Probably our rectory wasn't unique, but the only time the three assistants and the pastor communicated was at mealtime. In my three years there we never once prayed together—something that was so essential in the seminary. Wait, we did pray. The pastor would say, "Bless us, Lord, and these thy gifts which we are about to receive from thy bounty through Christ our Lord, Amen," before lunch and dinner. We'd usually go in to watch the six-thirty news after dinner, and maybe after the evening appointments we'd be together again for television at ten or ten-thirty. But no talking while watching television.

Meals could easily have been silent. I began to feel that I was forcing conversation, trying to get everybody talking. If we did talk, it never got around to anything that was happening in the parish. It would usually stem from something in the newspaper that day, a flood or rainstorm. Did you have a nice day off? or Where are you going tomorrow?

I would find any reason to skip meals, to make appointments at noon or at six and then eat with the housekeeper in the kitchen afterwards. It was like home; I would eat at her kitchen table.

When I got together with my classmates I found I wasn't alone in what was happening. One of my closest friends lived in a rectory where there was absolutely no communication from the pastor. There was a convent of sisters in the parish and they didn't have much more communication either. My friend found a sister he could communicate with and after one year he was married. I say if that guy had had love in his rectory he'd be an active priest today. If a man can have some communication in the place where he works and be even moderately happy in his working conditions, and therefore be happy with himself, he's not going to jump at the first thing that seems to offer relief.

I need love and affection. And I offered people the opportunity to show it to me. I used to put a lot of time into preparing my sermons. After Mass I'd go out to the front steps to greet the people, a very Protestant gesture some would think, but I would stand out there, let the people driving by see me, and be absolutely selfish. I knew I worked hard on the sermon, and if they said they got something from it I beamed.

Other things were at work too. It took me a year and a half out of the seminary to realize I had a lot of reserve strength. I was the guy who flunked out, and that was constantly at the back of my mind, but I found I had something to offer people. I became more and more secure and as I did I began to express myself more forcefully.

But it began to sink in that the junior man does most of the work in a rectory and he's supposed to smile and say, Yes, Father, to every request, assignment, Mass, service that comes his way. An aunt of mine who is a nun told me to talk only to priests about your frustrations, never share them with a layman. I soon learned that talking to some priests was like broadcasting news all over the diocese. With laymen I had more confidence it would go no further. When I had problems and I couldn't talk them out with anybody, I'd just get into my car and drive out to a Trappist monastery in Berryville, Virginia, forty miles out in the country, or else go down to the beach.

The first year and a half at the parish weren't all that bad. Then it was 1968 and *the* document came out, the Pope's proclamation on birth control. In Washington priests were speaking out and Cardinal O'Boyle was silencing them and throwing them out of rectories right and left. In Richmond there was a lot of ferment too. However, Bishop Russell handled the matter a bit more charitably and realistically. He called in a theologian who was going to talk about the whole business of birth control and especially conscience and tell us what we could and couldn't preach. I think this fellow was a little less conservative than the bishop had thought, and he left us with the idea that people could form their conscience about the birth control issue and that no edict could cover every instance.

To get up in the pulpit the next Sunday and preach on the Gospel would have been ridiculous, so I prepared my homily about birth control. The pastor also was trying to address the point, gathering documents like *Costi Conubi* that would support the Pope's position. My sermon certainly did not tell people to practice birth control, but rather was about conscience, which, as Cardinal Suenens once said, is "The intimate dialogue between God and man." Form your own conscience on what you must do. There were some icy stares when I greeted people after Mass that Sunday and some people remarked that it was a great sermon. I told them I hoped they were still around when the ball started to fall.

The ones who gave the icy stares were the ones who wrote or called the pastor, and those who said the sermon was good never spoke up. If I could just have had some letters written by those people who verbally agreed with my position, how it would have helped. The pastor got reactions from the reactionaries and he unfortunately felt they reflected what most of the people felt.

He had had some calls by the time my five o'clock Mass came around and just before Mass I saw him walk into the sacristy so he could listen to my sermon. And I wondered, Shall I give it or not? I decided, in conscience, I had no choice. I was not trying to disobey God or anybody else, but I had to say what I thought was right. The next morning he confronted me at breakfast and asked for a copy of the sermon; he wanted to send it to the bishop. He accused me of going directly against the Pope, the bishop, and against the sermon he himself had preached the day before.

My sermon never got sent to the bishop, but other things unfolded in later months. One afternoon I found a set of rules on my desk from the pastor that was directed to all the priests of the parish. I knew it was directed at me, because I was the one who was already "breaking" them. Beginning then, we were not allowed to bring anyone to our rooms except other priests and immediate family. I guess that would prevent any acts of—horrors!—fornication, because obviously no priest could be a homosexual. I'd regularly been bringing kids to the room after sweating out on the field to have a Coke or a casual talk. It was the best place for them to relax and just let go. Then there was something in the rules about the rectory being the living quarters of all the priests, and we all had to respect that and not come and go at late hours. I routinely had been coming in at eleven o'clock and on some nights even as late as midnight! And yet we were told that the rectory was our home.

Then there was a rule that whenever we left the rectory we had to put down where we were, the telephone number we could be reached at, and what time we'd be back. I went out once and put down where I was going but didn't put down the number. When I came back the number was on the bulletin board; the pastor obviously had looked it up. (Bishop Russell later told me he never demanded that of his curates.)

It was like the seminary all over again. You had to sneak to get around the rules, just to live. Two good friends of mine—they were nurses—came to church one Sunday morning and I asked them over for coffee after Mass. I had to get the coffee and discreetly bring them in and out just to have a visit. I didn't want to talk to them in the common room or the kitchen with everybody around. What kind of conversation can you have that way? Does a priest have to share his friends with the pastor or the assistants?

Living like that, I became very nervous, and when I'm nervous I don't eat. It was very evident to the parishioners that something was up and they began asking me why I was losing weight and why I seemed so edgy.

That's a point a lot of priests get to and they start looking for something that will lift the terrible burden. I began to think, At least if I had marriage it would be easier; I could share this burden with someone. A priest sees all the marriage problems and he knows that it isn't the be-all and end-all, but sometimes you see a soap opera or a commercial and you convince yourself that's what it's really like. We're terribly naïve people. There was a song, "Little Green Apples," that really used to get me because whenever the man needed her the woman was always there. "I get up in the morning . . ." and on it would go. It was phony, but it's so appealing to think of somebody being there just to say good morning to you.

Then it came through that maybe the priesthood wasn't for me. I need loving so much and I'm not getting it from anybody and maybe I've just got to get out.

Things had gotten to such a point that I told the pastor that maybe marriage was the answer, and he said, "Now, Father, we all have these impure thoughts." Missed the point completely. He told me to take more time off or to play golf and he invited me to go play golf with him. That was the answer to all the problems. It was stupid.

This was at the time when priests were leaving in great numbers and I just didn't know what to do. Maybe I just needed some time to stand back and see what this whole thing was all about. I went to the bishop and requested a leave of absence. He just couldn't see it; it had never been done before in the diocese. And anyhow, no man ever comes back if he takes a leave, he said.

I will, I promised him. I will keep you informed and I will come back. I'll write you and I definitely will keep in touch with other priests. When I left I wrote him a long letter. I remember the first line: "I know you're going to be heartbroken when you receive this letter, because I know you must get so many problems in the mail every day." And I told him I wasn't leaving because I disliked him or the priests but it was because the rectory structure had me so uptight and my physical condition was waning.

He could never say he didn't know what Dick Martin was doing, because I would always write him detailed letters, two or three single-spaced pages long; they make up a thick folder by now. He didn't quite know what to do about me, because I was the first priest to take just a leave and not a leave intending to marry. Since I was one of the first priests to take a leave for this reason, there were no rules or guidelines of what I was supposed to do or of what was expected of me while on this leave. Bishop Russell never ceased to be a truly kind man to me throughout my ordeal, although I knew that he never really understood the why of my actions. His letters back to me would often be just a paragraph four or five lines long, and in the beginning they were addressed to Mr. Richard B. Martin and started Dear Dick. In the middle it was Dear Father, and now they're addressed to Reverend Richard B. Martin and they begin Dear Dick. But what I was hoping through the correspondence was really to educate the man, to show him a priest can live on his own, that a priest can do good work, social work outside the church structure, that his place of residence was secondary. I don't know if I succeeded or not.

When I discussed my leaving with the bishop, I remember him

asking me if I said my breviary every day; that was the criterion for being a good priest, I guess. At the time I *was* saying it. The whole breviary business got to me anyhow. I can remember being in a car with a priest near midnight and he hadn't said it, so he turned the back light on and with the radio still on and while jumping in and out of the conversation, he said the breviary. I can remember priests sitting in front of TV sets looking at ballgames and saying the office. Still the criterion was that a good priest is the one who faithfully says his breviary. The guy who's out all day and falls into bed at night bushed and doesn't say it—he's not going to get the graces.

The bishop tried to reassign me to another parish, thinking that would solve all my problems. But the leave was a necessity, really, for my physical and mental well-being. If I had accepted a transfer, I would have had a nervous breakdown two weeks later. I'd been to a doctor and he told me that my health was deteriorating. But I was determined that I wasn't going to sneak out of the parish or leave without an explanation to the people I loved. This wasn't going to be one of those quiet seminary exits. I loved those people for three and a half years and I wanted them to know why I was leaving, and I didn't want vicious rumors to start that I was leaving for a woman.

On the last Sunday, December 1, 1968, I told my people that in conscience and justice to them and in light of Vatican II and the events that followed it, I had to take a step aside from my own priesthood and take another look at it. I told them I'd be living in the vicinity and that I'd be coming back periodically to the parish for worship. I didn't expect to be allowed to say Mass; I was ready to return to the pews as a worshiper.

I saved my parting words for after the Mass, because I was a little bit fearful that I might be stopped by the pastor if I said them in the midst of the Mass. Then I don't know, I felt filled with the Holy Spirit and I told the people in my own words how much I loved them and that I hoped they would pray for me. It was one of the most emotional moments of my life. We had a deacon, Tom Ryan, a Marist, and he had my car waiting in back of the church and I took off the vestments and dashed right out. It was too emotional a moment to stop and chat with people.

There was a man who caught me on the way out—I didn't even know him—and he said simply, "Father, do you have a place to stay tonight?" I wish I could find him. "Father, do you have a place to stay tonight?"

I went to my parents' home in Rhode Island and the next morning I woke up as Mr. Martin, feeling very insecure about it all. When something happens to one member of our family, everybody is upset; we are a "tight" family.

Dad felt hurt because of the instability that had entered my life at a time when he thought that I was settled. My mom, like all good mothers, was concerned over my health. I think I could have left the church but as long as I looked happy, was healthy, and smiled she would be content. Jack and Madeleine (my brother and sister) were always a source of strength, perhaps because there was no "generation gap." Throughout the whole four years, my family never ceased to always "be there." I have read of many men who have been almost disowned by their families because they have left the active ministry. Thank God for my good family, who, although I know they didn't agree with everything I was doing, were always there! I think it was because of their understanding and kindness and always making me feel welcome at home that I actually never abandoned the idea of priesthood altogether.

This state of being neither fish nor fowl didn't fit comfortably with me, because I really was quite a follower. I was the kind who would say, Yes, Father, to the pastor in the rectory; I really responded to church authority. I had the job in drug addict rehabilitation lined up, and I knew I would be starting soon, but I still had to make a new set of rules to live by. I had never lived without rules. But it didn't seem to make sense to make up rules yet, so I said to myself, I'm going to let my life evolve and see what comes of it.

The reaction to my leaving was interesting. I felt very close to the eight men I was ordained with, and I sent them a mimeographed letter explaining what I was doing and where I was living. A week or two before, they were my best friends and we were doing things together. I don't think I got one letter of support back. It was as if the prodigal son had left. But then something beautiful happened the following May 14, which was the anniversary of our ordination. Our class was to have a concelebrated Mass and, of course, I could not be part of that. One of my classmates, Father Majewsky from southern Virginia, said he was going to spend the day with me in Washington. We went out to dinner. We didn't say a Mass, but that man, reaching out in charity to me, said a greater Mass than the group in Richmond.

Among other priests, the most prominent feeling I got back was jealousy. The impression was that things were so easy now, that this guy Martin could just take off because he didn't like the parish he was in. It was like a parent saying, I had to go through this at your age and you have to go through it now. And yet there were people like Monsignor Carroll Dozier, who has since become Bishop of Memphis. He gave me the keys to his summer house in Virginia Beach, flew me down there, gave me his car, and just told me to rest and have a good time. He said he didn't want to hear any explanations.

In 1972 Father John Hannan, who might be thought of as a conservative as far as church matters go, asked me if I would say Mass each day for his nuns in the convent at Queen of Apostles in Alexandria. Up until that time I had been leaving home early each morning and going to the National Shrine of the Immaculate Conception in Washington, about ten miles away, to offer Mass in some little private chapel in the crypt. I never liked offering Mass in private (and still don't), but I felt this need to offer Eucharist and this was one way to satisfy that desire. My routine changed somewhat when I began saying Mass at Queen of Apostles Convent. I rose at five-thirty each morning, drove the six miles to Queen of Apostles from my apartment, said Mass for five sisters at six-forty-five, had a quick breakfast, and dashed to catch a seven-forty-five bus to get me to the city by eight-fifteen. With that schedule I was always wide awake by the time I began my day with my "kids." It certainly was proof enough for me that living apart from the rectory could work.

Another time Father Hannan heard I wasn't feeling so well and he said to come and live in the rectory for a week so I could get rest and three good meals and have somebody there to look after me. The liberals, the new school guys, didn't have much time for me. By God, I found you can be conservative but you can be kind.

When I started the leave I didn't have too many clothes (what I did have were "basic black") but I had more charge accounts than I knew what to do with. So I went to a very expensive store in Washington and charged a whole wardrobe. Then I charged my furniture and rented some more. Money was no barrier; in the parish I had a secure life and it was always easy to pay bills. I got $100 base pay a month, another $75 for what we called stole fees—funeral and wedding donations—and two or three dollars a day in Mass stipends. A month later, when all these secular bills came in, it dawned on me I knew nothing about budgeting money. I was like a little kid suddenly thrust into a world of apartment rent, utilities, laundry bills, and then the luxuries. Before I only had to pay for the luxuries.

I was making $8400, but knock off taxes and it came to $6000. Pay $150 for rent, and then take care of all the necessities and there wasn't much left. When I was in the parish we charged all our gas; now I was looking for the discount gas stations and putting in regular instead of high test. After seven or eight months I was finally able to afford a secondhand TV set for $68. Financial matters were eased considerably when a good friend of mine from home, Sergeant Bob Lapointe, then stationed at the Pentagon, decided to share the apartment and the expenses with me. Originally I remember allowing $15 of my budget for food every week. Now I could spread it over a two-week period. We didn't live high on the hog, but we didn't lose weight either.

I enjoyed my new life. I'd get up in the morning an hour earlier just to get the right clothes together. I enjoyed putting clothes on, yellows and blues and greens. I enjoyed getting on the bus in the morning and coming in to see friendly faces. And when five o'clock came I enjoyed leaving it all, knowing I could come back refreshed the next morning. In the rectory, you live, sleep, eat with the same three people and it can get on your nerves. I now believe that a priest should have a parish business place apart from his living quarters. Not that he can't be reached after five o'clock. A doctor is on call twenty-four hours a day, but he doesn't live at the hospital.

When I started my job I wanted to be the good Joe, and I went through a period where I took many of the girls to lunch. It always had been a Dutch treat system, but I didn't know that and they didn't know how to handle me any more than I knew how to act with them. My budget began to hurt.

I dated and I began to date one girl steadily. She loved the same things I did. Six or seven months into the leave of absence, we were together for a ride one day and she asked me point-blank what I was going to do with my life. She wanted to start her life and I think she did love me. I said, "I just don't know yet." She psyched me out right there. "You love your church and you're never going to leave it," she said. It was something right out of the movie *The Cardinal.* I couldn't deny what she was saying.

So if I knew before the end of the first year, why has it taken me four years to decide to come back to the active ministry? Why?

Because I was enjoying the freedom that I did not have in the rectory. I was enjoying doing all the little things that parishioners had to do but Father never had to. A man can be the worst priest in the diocese and he still has a roof over his head and meals every day. The outside world was a challenge. I was in a job where I had to make it work or I would starve.

Going to another level, I felt like the man in Francis Thompson's *Hound of Heaven.* I knew the hound was there, but I felt compelled to go up and down the beaten track. I ran and I ran, but the hound stayed right behind me, and I guess after four years I just got tired of running away from him. The only reason I would stay on the leave now would be to keep my independence. It wouldn't be because I'm 100 per cent fulfilled. I'm really not as fulfilled as I was in the active ministry. I have left one structure, but I am caught in another. The biggest fallacy among priests leaving is that they leave the structure behind. They can't. A couple other guys left the same time I did and we vowed we'd get together and create something new. But that fizzled out. The structures must exist; we just have to find new ways of using them.

Looking back, there wasn't a day in those four years that I didn't think about the priesthood in one form or another. And I tried everything possible to divorce myself from it. I'd call a priest or a nun and I'd say Mr. Martin was calling. But it just didn't work. I kept a picture on my desk at work of my sister Madeleine's wedding, with me in the background in my vestments. Through it all, I was proud of being a priest. When the addicts came I'd tell them who I was, and that led to more talks about religion than it had in the rectory.

I come back with a skill and I hope it will be utilized. I want to go into southern Virginia this time; in places like Norfolk they have halfway houses for addicts and delinquents and that would be an ideal place for me to work. Or in Catholic Charities or social development, anything where these four years of experience won't be wasted. If I have to, I'll reside in a rectory, but I really prefer not to be part of a parish structure right now.

I've learned so much I'd like to share with all the guys who are thinking of leaving the ministry. For one thing, if they must leave, they should wait at least a year, maybe two before getting married. I've seen so many frustrated priests who thought marriage would salve all the wounds. Or else men who have decent marriages but who are frustrated in the work they need to survive. Public relations for the telephone company, washing dishes, working in some government bureaucracy—these men are so unhappy and, I feel, so unfulfilled. They know what they left behind. A leave can be very beneficial; I would never automatically discourage any priest from taking time off.

I work with young people with problems here, but they know and I know they have to come to me because the courts say so, and if they behave and get a job they will be released from my jurisdiction. The work of the priesthood is still to get to the inner person. When he doesn't have to make any points with you, it's more of a mutual struggle. I feel people still have a basic respect for the clergy; they feel the priest is one of the last people they can go to when they're down and out and really talk things over without getting charged twenty bucks an hour. Here I have guys who come to me for legitimate needs: money or clothes or a job. In the parish, you oftentimes can offer them something deeper, something that could transform their whole lives, in addition to providing for their material wants.

I have an ex-priest friend who married right away, and every time I see him he can't stop telling me how happy his marriage is, yet the conversation always ends up on the priesthood. He's a frustrated priest, and I feel his marriage is not fulfilling him as much as his priesthood did. Many men who left to get married would come right back if they were allowed. So many have the gnawing feeling they're doing less than they're able to do, than they once did.

All I know is that the hound caught up with me and now I'm going back with fear and trepidation but also with a great deal of faith and hope. I realize I could be faced with the same situation I had four years ago. But it's almost as if there is a new guy ordained. I often say I pity the poor pastor that gets me for the next couple of years. I'm not going to disobey him just for the sake of it. But I'm going to be me, not some puppet with his stomach all knotted up inside. I want to serve where they can get the best use out of me, but I am going to know where I'm going before I hand in my resignation here. No blind faith. A team ministry would really appeal, working with two or three guys that really loved one another, were respected by one another, and were burning to get the work done. It's the wave of the future: priests will virtually marry each other and promise to give and share and work together for the needs of the people. Or priests living in communities and going out each day to their separate jobs.

Regardless of what I do, I hope the bishop will allow me to help him in talking with or trying to help guys thinking of taking a leave of absence. I can't think of a person better qualified. I'll be the first one to tell a man to take a leave of absence if he's having his doubts. I'll be the first one to tell him not to get married immediately.

I'm going back strangely convinced that instead of discarding the clerical dress we as priests should keep it—especially during professional work hours. Off hours I see no reason why the priest cannot clothe himself in whatever styles and colors he sees fit, including suit and tie. When meeting with other professional men, however, I think the collar is the only appropriate dress at this time. If it changes in the future I'll be the first to go along with it. From working with professional men in my job here at rehabilitation I have reached the conclusion that many priests don't think of themselves as professional men, and just as many don't act it.

Priests and nuns are still signs in the world and we need signs with all the turmoil we have. You see a nurse and she's an external sign of something. Religious should be the same way, a visible sign of what they stand for and what they should be expected to practice. And I'm going back convinced that—although they told us differently in the seminary—life is not a vale of tears and we are not all worthless residents of the planet. A young sister in our parish told me four years ago not to leave, that didn't I know I was a sensitive, loving person, and people felt it? I said no. Now I can say yes. After four years I can answer the question *yes.* I never had any idea that I had worth as a person alone until I was able to put myself out in the marketplace and make it, that I could be complimented for work and not automatically praised because I sported a white Roman collar.

There just must be some reason why I came through all this. I had a wonderful Franciscan professor in seminary, Father Augustine Tor, who always insisted that a seat in the class be left vacant. It was for Christ, he said. He wrote me that each age has its prophets, its pioneers. And that perhaps because I didn't go along the normal channels and although I really wasn't sure what I was about, perhaps—without sounding presumptuous—I was one of those prophets or pioneers.

August 1, 1972

The Most Reverend John J. Russell, D.D.
807 Cathedral Place
Richmond, Virginia

Dear Bishop Russell:

After giving this letter much thought, prayer and reflection I would like to share with you the following concerning my transfer to full ministry within the diocese.

In 1969 I requested a leave of absence because of the pressures of rectory living at that time. At *no* time did I consider a leave because I did not like the work of the priesthood. During this time I have continued to offer Mass and presently offer daily Eucharist at Queen of Apostles Church. At that time (1969) there was no personnel committee to turn to as there is now—a committee which I feel is of tremendous importance to priests of today.

I began working as a counselor for Social Rehabilitation and in particular with the Youth Services Division. Many types of young men and women have come to me, from the drug addict and the alcoholic to the school dropout and those from broken and troubled homes. These people always knew that I was a Catholic priest. Last fall I was asked to head a new program with the halfway houses here in Washington—the first such program under the newly enacted Youth Crime Act approved by Congress. I felt proud to be its first head counselor. During my time here at Rehabilitation I have also received several promotions, which clearly illustrate the confidence that the agency places in me.

The time "away" has truly been a mixed blessing. It has been a true learning experience that unfortunately I am not that adept at putting onto paper. I have seen firsthand the attitudes, anxieties, and difficulties that the laity must go through. The priesthood can easily become such a secure life that we priests can easily forget the value of the dollar and the difficulties confronting our people daily. This time has been like a practical course in psychology—only a better one than that taught at the university level—and seen from a different vantage point.

Hopefully the tone of this letter will not appear demanding or lacking in respect to you or to your office. Pope John said in his journal, "There are but two important things in life—one to know yourself and the other to love God." I feel that this time has truly helped me to know Dick Martin better and hopefully to bring back a much more mature and whole person than previously. It has also made me so much more aware of the beauty of the Eucharist in my life. At this point I would like to present the following to you.

As stated above, I was asked to head a new program within the halfway houses. At the end of the year I will have been in the position for one year, at which time it should be well on its own. At that time (December) I would like to hand in my resignation and be available for full-time service within the diocese four to six weeks thereafter (the time needed to transfer and settle cases).

Although I have benefited greatly from the work that I have been doing, I have come to appreciate priesthood even more so and to anticipate my return to full service as much as prior to ordination. My return to the active ministry is so strong that none of the attachments—including my $14,000 salary—seem as attracting.

I have been in contact with Bishop Sullivan, Vicar of Priests, and most recently visited with Father Pitt, head of the Priest Personnel Committee. It is with Father Pitt that I inquired about the possibility of being assigned to the Norfolk area of our diocese. Hopefully the experience I have gained here with Rehabilitation can be put into similar use either in a parish or school setup. I do not think that the needs and the problems of the youth of the Tidewater area are much different from those of the Washington area.

I was happy to learn several months ago after the completion of a survey of our priests that it was proposed that various life styles be investigated. I would appreciate being considered for such an experiment if it were inaugurated within our diocese. Realistically it will not solve all of the problems of the priesthood, but I think that it would begin to solve a few and hopefully alleviate some of the frustration.

I would be remiss in this letter if I failed to mention the kindness of several priests whose encouragement has kept me close always to my priesthood, beginning with Bishop Carroll Dozier. Also I have always been impressed with the fraternalism and the optimistic answers to my letters which Bishop Sullivan has shown me. Lastly Father Hannan, who has shown me true charity by inviting me to offer daily Eucharist at his parish church and convent.

Lastly in this letter but first in importance to me has been your own kindness to me, Bishop. I know that my actions of 1969 were not fully understood by you (and many others) but I have always felt that you have been beside me as a father with his troubled son always trying to show me charity. For this I want to sincerely thank you, Bishop. In time there is growth, and I feel that we both have grown through this experience. I would like to think that it is your continued promise of prayers for me that has led me to write to you at this time. I hope, Bishop, that this letter will be most welcome to you. Undoubtedly you would have preferred it coming sooner. Nevertheless, Bishop, I am a firm believer in Providence and feel strongly that in all of this and throughout these years that God's hand was ever present.

Appreciating your continued concern for my priesthood, I remain,

Sincerely in Christ,
(Rev.) Richard B. Martin

part two

The System: On Whose Authority?

"I realized for the first time that I was an orphan, that I didn't have a big white father any more telling me what to believe, what was right and wrong. Because if the Pope was wrong on that point, then he could be wrong on anything. I truly believed the Spirit would wither the Pope's hand before something like that could be written."

—Father Donald Ranly

"To me the church, the priesthood, is still the frame of reference I need to work from. I'll bypass the rigamarole, the excess baggage, the needless paraphernalia which the simple structure that Jesus instituted did not include."

—Father Francis Eschweiler

"I don't know if it's a lack of confidence of faith on the part of us bishops as though if we looked at a problem it would overwhelm us. Don't we have enough confidence that even though Jesus may be asleep in the boat, he's there and he can lead us through? We're men of little faith who, when you get right down to it, rather than deal with problems, run for cover. And I suppose at some point Jesus is going to wake up and rebuke us. I hope he does."

—Bishop Thomas Gumbleton

"It no longer is a big enormous threatening thing to get out of this whole chaos that is the institutionalized church. I've had four or five years without all those institutional buttresses and platforms and tentacles. It's not a success trip of course, and the real difficulty and the real purpose is still to steal the book back for the people. If I have any vocation or vision at this point, that's about what it is. Because Cardinal Cooke owns the book, owns the meaning of religion right now."

—Father Joseph O'Rourke

Father Donald Ranly

Father Donald Ranly's life is lived out of a series of storefronts in East Chicago, Indiana. East Chicago, with its putrid air and grimy buildings, is the home of refineries, mills, and tens of thousands of people who are forced into a not-so-pleasant coexistence with the industries that employ them. In this city Don Ranly (1) teaches journalism and speech at St. Joseph's Calumet College, whose face to the public is a series of storefronts along Indianapolis Boulevard, (2) lives in a tiny apartment converted from a storefront, and (3) spends a great amount of his time at Harbor House, the once-deserted storefront that he made into an overnight shelter for the bums, winos, and passers-through.

East Chicago promised jobs, security, a better way of life to workers many years ago, but somehow the city has gone sour, turned on them, reneged on its promise. For Don Ranly, who at the age of fourteen entered the Society of the Precious Blood's minor seminary with similar hopes, the priesthood and the church have gone sour, turned on themselves.

The last of sixteen children of a family raised on a puny farm in Cassella, Ohio—an area more thoroughly Catholic than the Vatican itself—Don was the spoiled and pampered one. The Ranlys were a religious family. Two of his brothers and one of his sisters had already gone into the religious life. His mother coaxed, cajoled, even bribed young Don with the vague promise of "somehow getting the money" to send him to medical school so he wouldn't go to the seminary.

He was a precocious, intelligent boy who easily led his grade school class. Today two fingers on his right hand are shorter—like broken pickets in a fence—because of his inquisitiveness. In the fifth grade he stuck a finger in the family's meat grinder to see if it would grind human flesh. It did. In the eighth grade he was trying to figure out how he had done it and ground down another finger.

At first he cried at the seminary that put him in a cassock and wouldn't let him go home until the next summer, but something kept him there and brought him back. Don Ranly was beginning to enjoy the intellectual challenge of school and studies. He was beginning to read and to write, and eventually he became the editor of virtually every seminary publication.

As ordination day in 1962 approached, Don Ranly had already had papers published. In one he argued forcefully for the sharing of the Communion cup at weddings, quoting scripture and citing practices of primitive tribes who drank each other's blood and of American Indians who opened their veins to each other to form a more perfect bond. The church was ripe for change and he was excited to be part of that change as a priest, preacher, writer, and pastor.

As a young priest he bowed to authority; he took his vow of obedience seriously. But then events of the 1960s erupted. While studying in Milwaukee he began to write about an unknown white priest from a black parish, Father James Groppi. Don Ranly began to see the response from the church to which he had sworn his allegiance and vowed his service. Catholics counterdemonstrated against Groppi with a bier bearing a likeness of the priest with a knife plunged into his chest and the words "A good Groppi is a dead Groppi." He waited for the church hierarchy to respond to this man who seemed to Ranly to be cut from the mold of Old Testament prophets. Silence. Condemnation. Threats.

After two years of teaching at his order's backwoods seminary Ranly studied one summer at New York University, and during euphoric days in Greenwich Village he sorted out the reality and the mystique of his priesthood. He was angry that he had swallowed Catholic doctrine and angry he had responded to its insensitive authority. By the time he got to East Chicago the circle had almost been completed, but one Pavlovian response was gone in the Greening of Don Ranly. He would no longer salivate at the tinkle of the bell of church authority. Today, at age thirty-eight, torn by his love-hate relationship with the church, it is a day by day struggle for Don Ranly to stay in the priesthood.

I always thought I was realistic about the church. After all, with my brothers Vic and Ernie as priests, I knew what they had to go through and what they did. But did I know what I was doing at fourteen when I first went in? Hardly.

The intellectual part of seminary life captivated me from the start; I kept on insisting I was getting a first rate education, and perhaps I was. But what the seminary did and did beautifully was destroy our sense of imagination, our questioning. It gave us all the answers and threw us into the Catholic bag. I swallowed the church totally (we used to call that "having faith"), learned all the justifications to make dogma stick so that the Gospel was lost in the process. I really believe this: so much theology, so much of the seminary worked to complicate and obscure the Gospel.

I guess every seminarian goes through stages. Save the natives in Brazil this year, and next year mysticism, and why not be another Thomas Merton, live in a cell, get up at three in the morning to chant the office. I seriously weighed the contemplative life. During the novitiate I sat down and read forty spiritual classics, books like Thomas à Kempis's *Imitation of Christ*, books by St. Thérèse, St. Teresa, St. John of the Cross, St. Francis de Sales. And I liked what I was reading. But just recently I looked over that list and realized that another book I read a couple of years later had far more impact on me. *Sister Carrie* by Theodore Dreiser. By God, that book turned my guts. This rich guy who got himself a whole bagful of money that wasn't his and ended up in flophouses and died in skid row. It was about the same time that I heard about Dorothy Day and the Catholic Worker movement, and something was planted there.

So much for my retrospective spiritualism. In 1962 I started off my priesthood by reading the Gospel of Jesus Christ with my back to the people of God, mumbling in a foreign language. I was taught, and I believed, that if I said, "This is my body"—in Latin, of course—loud enough for anyone to hear, it was a mortal sin. Catholics forget those "good old days." People wondered why priests looked down when they turned to the congregation to say, "Dominus vobiscum." It was a venial sin to look at the people!

In the first year of my priesthood, at a church in Detroit, I played the young priest role well and obediently, saying to myself I needed the experience. I sat in confessionals for three hours on Saturday afternoons hearing people grope for a way to express how evil they'd been since their confession last week. I got paid twenty bucks for those hours, while the pastor was up in his room watching Notre Dame football. And the twenty bucks wasn't coming out of his pocket. It was out of the pockets of the poor, pathetic, guilt-ridden people that lined up for Confession.

I said three Masses on Sunday so that the pastor and his assistant could say one and take off for the afternoon at the lake. I started seeing it was all right for a priest to have a yacht, a cottage at the lake, and a big car; but he couldn't have a girl and, of course, he didn't have to relate to those peasants who were his parishioners. I was used just like every other young priest was used. A pastor would pat me on the back. "Great sermon, Father Ranly. I'd really like you to do our Lenten series. And maybe you could give a hand with religious education. You're so good with the young people." Then he'd sit in the rectory and watch TV. He wasn't up on the latest things, he'd confess, hadn't read, hadn't had the time. "But, Father Ranly, right out of the seminary, you can really give them the most recent stuff." I ran into a man who gave nothing but retreats and missions, and he admitted he hadn't read a book in sixteen years.

When I went to Marquette for further study, it was as though I'd been rescued from twenty years in some intellectual and spiritual vacuum. I started on a master's degree in journalism in 1963 and began writing for the Milwaukee diocesan paper, *The Catholic Herald Citizen*. A friend of mine was down in Selma for the marches and sent me a picture of—by God—a Milwaukee priest. And we printed his picture captioned by something to the effect that Milwaukee had a priest with soul. Nobody knew the name or the face then. It was Jim Groppi.

Groppi came back and organized marches, and I covered them like an eager cub reporter fascinated with this white priest amidst the blacks and the fine Catholics demonstrating against him, calling for his head. At first it was just interesting and good copy, but then as I saw Groppi on one side, virtually pitted against the Catholics, it became clearer. Groppi was saying the right things, and on the other side I could see the disease; we had trained people to be Catholic and nothing else. Catholics were the ultimate Pharisees. They stood for the very thing that Christ condemned: narrow-mindedness, closed-offness from any other people or any other point of view.

During the days in Milwaukee I saw that the Word wasn't being lived out. For instance, take the St. James Epistle. If a man comes up to you hungry and you say, Go your way, brother, I'll pray for you, that isn't really where it's at. Faith must be lived through our good works. I began to see that the guy sequestered in his comfortable rectory or in a damp cell someplace was just kidding himself. Scourging yourself instead of going out and feeding your brother—that's a real distortion. Really, it's horseshit.

Groppi was just terribly right, the right place, the right time. And then the auxiliary bishop told him to stop. I don't want to come off as some kind of coach of somebody like Jim Groppi, but I called him and told him he couldn't stop. There were higher things, that he should tell the bishop to go to hell. That time Jim stopped.

It wasn't too long after this that the same bishop was out at the convent where I was living, ready to say his Mass and in an absolute rage. Why? The nuns wanted to sing part of the Mass! The next thing, he said, they're going to want part of the stipend. As I went to school that day I saw him get into a Buick, a big black Buick with a priest chauffeur. And I just said to myself that this is the last time in my life I'm ever going to defend that kind of junk, the last time I'm going to pretend that a man like that makes sense, the last time in my life I'm going to justify respecting or "obeying" a man who has no sense of dignity, no intelligence, no nothing, just because he wears a bishop's ring. Never was I going to accept authority because it was authority. And I thank that bishop for clearing my head.

I loved Pope John and I thought he was going to take us away from all that, but on the diocesan level I just couldn't see it. In the light of an allegedly changing church, men like this bishop were telling us priests that they were serious. I can condemn and condemn and what does that benefit me? I don't know, except that there is a continuing pretense on the part of these men, that they claim to be some special kind of descendants of Jesus Christ. And they have the right to tell me whom I can live with, whom I can sleep with, and whom I can love. Either I have to go on under the pretension of giving them accolades and deference, acting as if I respect them, looking to them for leadership—or I opt out.

I saw mammoth rectories, convents, and seminaries being emptied as the exodus of religious got under way. And I saw rescue missions in the inner city jammed with people who literally had no place to stay. I gave retreats to nuns during the Milwaukee years, and the stories of inhumanity are plentiful. A couple comes to the convent in the middle of the night and a nun opens the door, hears that they are destitute, and knows that all she can do is direct them to the Salvation Army. Then her mother superior chews her out for even letting the people come in. Or the mother superior who made a nun wash the entire bathroom with Lysol after some black friends of hers came to visit. Didn't she know what kind of diseases those kind of people communicated?

Nearly everywhere I turned, the church's inhumanity bombarded me. Nuns in the convents? Hell, I know this sounds sensational, but I couldn't believe how many nuns slept with each other. I don't know how much of it was lesbianism; it was just that these suppressed women were dying to have somebody hold them, to experience human affection. Oh, the old ones would say, "Father, Sister, you knew what you were doing when you came into the religious life." Lock up a guy or a girl at fourteen and say all that dramatic language to them and do you think they are able to make a rational choice?

I don't mean to say that all my years and experiences in the priesthood have been bad or bitter. As a matter of fact, in the first years I was saying I had sold the priesthood short. It was a good profession, I was a professional, I did my work well and liked it. I had great consolations in the confessional and on retreats.

But then I came to realize that I spent over three-fourths of my time relieving people of guilt that the church had imposed upon them! Getting people out of their Catholic bag! Telling them that much of what their pastors and grade school nuns had taught them was a bunch of crap!

I began to question whether I truly liked celebrating the Mass and preaching or whether I simply liked the stage. I made good theater, even in Latin. And the people loved me, especially nuns, women. So many women oohed and aahed and so many of them told me they hoped I would never marry. I suddenly realized that I was a vestal virgin, that I would have been more free to serve as a married man, that many of these women would not have come to me had I been married.

Celibacy stands as the monument to the utter and complete inhumanity of the church. It is a deprivation of a basic human right, and eventually I have come to a point where I actually think for a person at a certain stage in life to say, I will never fall in love with someone enough to commit myself in marriage, is immoral.

Internally, during the four years in Milwaukee, I had developed a rejection of church authority and it was beginning to show. Near the end I started participating in demonstrations instead of just reporting them. I remember picketing the chancery because the bishop refused to let the Catholic schools be freedom schools during the boycott. A couple of us did it with collars on and we heard that we were going to get the boot. But nothing ever happened. That's frustrating too, when you can't even get a reaction from the people you're screaming at.

So, from this fantastic arena of activity and schooling in Milwaukee, I ended up in 1967 at our seminary in Carthagena, a little country place two miles from the farm I was raised on. I was at a point where I thought confrontation was the answer, and it wasn't long before I was confronting. Christ said a prophet is not accepted in his own land—wow!

I helped formulate one anti-war letter and signed it along with seventeen seminarians. We sent it to all the papers around there including one that my brother worked for. American Legion man, very patriotic, he let me know that he won the war for me and that if I didn't like it here I should go to Moscow. I was editor of the *Precious Blood Messenger* and I did a cover story on Vietnam showing some Vietnamese kids hiding in a trench with the soldiers. And underneath in khaki-colored letters, "May Christians Kill?" The cancellations poured in, the letters: "When are you priests going to teach us how to save our souls and stop getting political?" The furor just made me ask, Where had I been? What had taken me so long? How could I talk from a pulpit about loving my neighbor and feeding the hungry and yet justify killing, stand by justifying murder?

For two years I had a weekly forty-five-minute radio show. I brought on Judge So-and-so, political party people, Elks, Moose, Knights, Masons. And I just asked them questions about some of the problems that the area and the country were into. And back came these racist statements, these flat declarations backing war and capital punishment. Christians, Catholics almost exclusively. I got into the migrant scene—lots of tomato pickers down there—and saw a good Catholic lady go to work as a nurse every morning at Mercy Hospital, and within twenty feet of her house were five shacks that had one water spigot between them. Babies being born in chicken coops, toilets without a light, with a floor your shoes stuck to.

The good monsignor told us, "Now when you go to visit these camps, your job is not to inspect them; you're there to teach catechism." I was supposed to go into those camps and show them a flick on Confirmation on the back of a chicken coop and then pack up and leave.

Bernard Cooke* said that Martin Luther King didn't cause hatred, he just exposed it. Through the radio program, the magazine, through a weekly newspaper column where for four years I never resorted to anything but concrete examples, I tried that: to expose hatred. But *I* was hated.

I can get terribly paranoid about this whole thing, but then

* Cooke, a respected Jesuit theologian, has left his order and married. He is still active in church circles and writes for many religious and secular periodicals.

when I do look back I don't think I can really remember how bad it was. Then the crucial blow was that I saw the very seminary where I was teaching as a pathetic example of what the church stood for. A faculty of ten teaching thirty-two seminarians in a building that housed a hundred when I had gone through. One man teaching all four years of moral theology, one man teaching all the Scripture. That place had operated for over a hundred years; I loved it. And I saw that I had to work to put it to death.

I can still remember one day during the last year at the seminary —it was the day Charles Davis left the priesthood—when I went down to the priests' recreation room (of course, priests, brothers, and seminarians were segregated) and there was this fierce argument between two of the men on Pope Paul's stand on birth control. *Humanae Vitae* had condemned birth control! I had worked out birth control very carefully, showing that the old premises were wrong, ridiculous, that the difference was that we were human beings and not natural animals. Suddenly a man, a Pope, who after having the best scholars work on the problem, rejects their findings and tells them (and me) we're wrong. When it sunk in that somebody was asking me to believe something and teach it only because he said so, that was traumatic. His authority transcended reason. I would never teach *Humanae Vitae*.

I realized for the first time that I was an orphan, that I didn't have a big white father any more telling me what to believe, what was right and wrong. Because if the Pope was wrong on that point, then he could be wrong on anything. I truly believed the Spirit would wither the Pope's hand before something like that could be written. Infallible teaching? One theologian said that the encyclical was not infallible but it was the work of the Holy Spirit! Think about that for a while! The Pope is infallible but the Holy Spirit isn't! That's the kind of nonsense church authorities were spouting. For a while you had to go to Canada to practice birth control. And who suffered? The ordinary believing Catholic!

I drove to my mother's home and said, "Mom, I am not going to be a priest very long because they're going to make me teach this and I'm not going to teach it. I will never teach it until I'm convinced of it, and I don't think that's going to happen."

"No, Don, you'll never get in that kind of trouble."

I told her again, "I owe it to you to tell you, Mom, I'm not going to say what they want and if they throw me out I'm not fighting."

She's really kind of neat, because she didn't say anything then, but a couple of weeks later I was leaving the house and she stuck her head out the window. "Now, you listen to the Pope. He's still your boss."

I really knew I was a pilgrim; the pilgrim church idea never hit me till then. I was a wayfarer like every Hindu, Moslem, Methodist, Lutheran, looking for the truth. I caught on that when Pope Paul cries about "losing faith," he means faith in him, in authority.

Before that it appealed to me to point to men like Cardinal Newman to show this was truly Christ's church; it had infallibility. Newman's whole argument was based on his belief that God couldn't have a church without an infallible spokesman. I liked certitude. If this was Christ's church it speaks the truth, and I felt sorry for the guy who didn't have it.

When I threw out the church's infallibility and authority, then other things fell by the wayside. Hell went out as a possibility. Christ had called on me to forgive my brother—alcoholic, thief, dope addict. Wouldn't God do the same? No longer did it make sense to do anything in life to avoid hell. It wasn't there. I just know that if God wants to damn me to hell for anything I do, then I say, God damn Him; I'll have nothing to do with Him, nothing.

The seminary was closing down and there was a lot of bitterness going around. Closing it was the right thing to do, but it hurt everybody. I just knew I had to get out of the seminary bag if I wanted to keep my sanity. I got offers to teach at other seminaries, but I knew I couldn't. One day the dean threw this brochure into my box from New York University on a six-week summer course in film, radio, and television. I didn't know where I was going, but I had to get out and this looked interesting as an interim step.

I was in this little town of Donaldson, Indiana, a few weeks later, giving a retreat to the Poor Handmaids of Jesus Christ. And I went directly from there to Greenwich Village to start the course. Before, I had played the clergy role so carefully, wouldn't be seen without a Roman collar. For the opening get-together of our class at NYU I wore a tie for the first time in my life. I introduced myself as Father Ranly, told them I wanted to be called Don, and off I went. The suit and tie went too, and from that day I wore a sloppy worn T-shirt, rubber thongs, and an old baggy pair of pants. We were told to; we were working with dusty studio equipment and we put in long days.

I'm a Scorpio and I've never been known for my moderation. Even when other guys were quitting saying the office, I religiously stayed with it, knowing that if I made an excuse today I'd find another tomorrow and it would slip away. But at NYU I just stopped cold, and I didn't have the least feeling of guilt. It was a ridiculous practice I had let go on too long. But I realized how much I believed "God would get me" if I did something "wrong" like not saying the breviary. I functioned very well without it.

I went over to the Newman Center and asked if it was possible for me to say Mass. Well, I'd have to make an appointment and see Monsignor about it. How late did the center stay open? I asked. Five o'clock in the summer. Five o'clock! This brand new beautiful air-conditioned fantastic building sat there virtually unused. I never went back. A deacon friend, Pat Fitzgerald—he's since married—and I got a bottle of wine and a loaf of bread on July 1, the feast of the Precious Blood, and just sat in our room and we liturgized. We sought out passages in Scripture on the significance of blood and we had a real Mass. Afterwards we just finished off the bottle of wine and went to bed. It was beautiful.

That was the only Mass I said in the six weeks. I did go to Mass every Sunday and found it a gruesome thing. If more priests would go to Mass and see how horrible it is I think they'd change. I went from church to church and got the same feeling: What has this got to do with anything? What I saw was what Bishop Pike saw in England: the death rattle of the Church of England. Old people and half-filled churches.

But what I really found out was that I didn't even miss the Mass. I didn't miss the whole damn business of religion. I knew from that time on it would be so much crap to tell somebody they really needed that. What right did I have to create in people a dependence on something like that? All the stuff I thought was so essential to my life was purged in those six weeks. The hypocrisy, the wealth, the stupidity of the leadership—it all came home as never before. And I could live without Communion, meditation, Confession. I lived pretty well, got A's in my courses, met a girl who was damn rich and probably could have married her, could have stayed on in New York and gone places. I suddenly knew I didn't *need* the church.

So why didn't I leave right then? Why didn't I? God, what a question. In one sense I might have let myself go that far because I knew it was ending in six weeks. On the other hand, two more weeks and I might have had it. And I would have been gone, and never would have set foot in another church. That would have been tragic, to leave as bitter as I was. Two things I hung on to during those six weeks: "a Christ thing"—there was something in this man that was still central to my life—and prayer. I could still talk to God. But all the trappings fell away. New York marks the end of Phase II of my life; Phase I ended in Milwaukee, and now I'm in Phase III. And, by God, it's got to be better.

After NYU all I was sure of was that I had to get away from seminaries, church things, and that's how I came to East Chicago.

I chose this place, this school, because I felt I had to start doing real things for real people. And it had to be in the city. Calumet

College is run by our order—but the last two presidents left the priesthood to get married. I made a few conditions before coming, to make sure that I could keep the church at a distance. I wanted my own apartment, so I wrote them I wanted "a crummy apartment." Never again will I live with another man, never, never, never. As I reflected on community life, I thought the Carthusians do it right. They live in their little cells and come together for prayer and meals. I found it with priests, I found it even more so with the nuns—physical proximity is more detrimental to community than contributory. All of your physical and psychic energy goes into trying to get along with everybody, and you feel guilty if you don't spend five minutes with each member each day. What religious men and women need is a sense of security and acceptance, and so often when you come back to a rectory or convent that's when you have the real hassle.

I came here in 1969, and I was beginning to feel that the time for confrontation, for me at least, was past. Even before I left the seminary I spoke to Brother John, a religious brother and close friend, about starting a house for the poor. I had seen Dorothy Day's work on the Bowery in New York and I had gotten to know Mike Cullen, who started Casa Maria, a Catholic Worker house in Milwaukee.* I came back from the big march in Washington in 1969 totally convinced that peacemaking was our task, the clear priority, the number one call of the Gospel at that time.

I knew I needed credibility too if I wanted to talk about peacemaking. I had to be a witness—not just a mouthpiece. I have a banner: "Make Peace, Be Kind." Kindness was the only word left that had any meaning to it. It's so easy to hate the haters. In *In the Heat of the Night* Sidney Poitier says, "I'll get those bastards,"

* Ranly has written a book about Cullen's life in Ireland, studies for the priesthood, emigration to America, participation in a draft file burning incident for which he served nine months in jail, and his house in Milwaukee. *A Time to Dance, the Mike Cullen Story,* as told to Don Ranly, 1972, The Messenger Press, Celina, Ohio.

and a slow smile comes over the face of Rod Steiger and he says, "You're just like us." Fantastic. You realize *when you hate the hater* you are just as bad as he is.

It's not that my transition from confrontation to an attempt at peacemaking was all that clean or abrupt. I was at war with myself. While I was talking about the house for the poor I was on the Lake County Committee to End the War in Vietnam; I was getting Rennie Davis in to speak; I was still demonstrating and confronting, just because of the futility I felt that nothing was changing. And again the support came from outside the church; church people wanted no part of it, and the people involved wanted no part of any church. Some people were alive in East Chicago. What a relief from Carthagena! People would listen if you spoke sense. Down in Ohio their brains were cast in concrete. Oh, Catholicism! So much self-righteous concern about abortion, but it was "necessary" to bomb the hell out of "Commies," even women and children.

I knew that I had to do something to change my whole orientation, because it became apparent that in a whole lot of areas if and when I spoke for something there was a good chance of it not happening, of my hurting the cause. I have a way of antagonizing people, and I knew I had to change before I could ask them to be any different.

Harbor House was, in a sense, my way of saying, I'll give the church one last chance. I'm going to see if I can get real people to do real things. And on another level it was a front. I wanted to "do" peace so I could talk about it. I couldn't really be against violence when I didn't see and do something about the violence inflicted on the hungry man and to the man who couldn't find a bed to sleep in. If I established Harbor House, by God, and established it well, regardless of being a wild man who talked about peace and no brutality, people could not deny that I was a guy who was doing something practical about it.

I was an organization man. It would have been easy for me to sit down and draw up a plan, by-laws, and just start Harbor House. But I sensed that wasn't the way. Maybe there was an element of faith lurking way, way in the background, so I decided to let it evolve, let it happen naturally with people who thought something like this was needed.

People just started popping up. I made a Cursillo*—by the way I think Cursillos have turned more Catholics into Christians than any other single experience—and came across this gambler. He was there because some guy by the name of Larry Field was making the rounds of the harbor bars telling people about Cursillos. So I found this Larry Field and told him about the house I wanted to start, and he lit up like a kid getting a lollipop.

We had a meeting, maybe ten people, and we found out about these empty storefronts right around the harbor bars, right in the middle of things. I didn't even see them and I said, Great, rent a place. We passed the hat and got the $50 for the first month's rent and that's the last time we paid. They could throw us out any day; no lease, no nothing. The storefronts were really in bad shape, abandoned six years previously by the Salvation Army! Big snowdrifts inside, no plaster on the walls. It looked great to me: I visualized beds in here, kitchen there, living room here. The other guys shook their heads and thought I went off my rocker when I walked through the place.

We had no money, no real plan, but we started. A guy named Tony Maicher said we had to panel the place, so he and another guy went over to a lumber company and got $400 worth of paneling for $90. Then two other guys went over to the local steelworkers' union, told them what we were doing, and walked out with a check for the $90. We got our first beds in, and our first guest was

* A Cursillo, "a little walk with Christ," is of Spanish origin, combining some group dynamics with Scripture, liturgy, and fundamental Christian concepts—Christ is your brother, your brother is Christ.

a guy who swore he was on his way to the Vatican to see the Pope. Okay, swell. We bummed a heater from Urban Redevelopment, got the water lines opened and started the begging. And by God, everything came! We got free plumbing, furniture, a deep freeze, kitchen equipment. The absolutely incredible thing was that we could get anything, anything we wanted. I got very mystical about the going out in twos as Christ sent them out. The whole spirit of the thing overwhelmed me. Never with the collar on did I feel that sure or have that much faith. I *knew* we could get what we needed when I went out with another person, simply stated our case and asked.

But we had feast and famine. We were loaded one day with two hundred loaves of bread and the next day we ran out of toilet paper. The inconsistency of it was draining. But when we asked, we got. Our little board, which I deliberately chose from mill types, settled down to the mystical twelve, and that size group worked pretty well.

As the whole thing developed and I spent more time at Harbor House I really found out how much I loved it. It's a hell of a lot simpler to work down there. I could really see why Jesus loved to be with sinners. These guys weren't truthful. Rotten liars, right to your face. But you knew that they weren't truthful and they knew you knew and there's something unpretentious about that. They tested the very fiber of your being, but it was good honest testing, not the ecclesiastical backbiting, the petty authority games that go on in the church. We have one guy named Blackie who will go to our chapel services so he can repeat my sermon back to me when I want to throw him out. Donald Duck stops driving his cab, goes on a bender, and knows that he can sleep at Harbor House. And when he gets sick he'll puke down the stairs instead of taking a few more steps to get into the john.

From the start I refused to make the place a mission where guys would have to attend services if they wanted a bed or meal. They already feel guilty, and you want them to believe God hates them too? The place didn't have so much as a crucifix in it, and one day I found somebody had put up this really sick picture of the Blessed Virgin, the really old-style Mary. I got it off the wall one night and put it on the front seat of my car and that night the car was stolen. I never saw the car or the picture again.

I continued to fight against any formal religious expression in the house, but the other board people—probably because of their Catholic upbringing—kept on pushing for a chapel and Mass. So we carved the chapel out of the damp basement and started having these Masses. My excuse for the chapel was to have a place for evicted families. At first three or four people would come—hardly ever the guests, only the real con artists attend—then it grew and we were having thirty or forty and CCD classes would come down and it turned into a real show, an In thing. Catholics! In a flophouse! We'd spend hours talking about how we were going to reach a guy and then we'd pray about it. The prayer thing became very, very real. I really learned a lot about prayer in that damp basement.

In no way could I escape it. This is where this Christianity business counts. Hindus, Moslems, I don't know of any philosophy that brings it all to bear. Like Sandburg said, If you see a child, you must name him all children.

I am so erratic that maybe tomorrow I'll quit Harbor House, priesthood, everything. But one thing for sure, never in my life will I say that the Gospel doesn't work. Never will I say you can't live that way. Never will I say that Christ's invitation is impossible—to come free of all the crap of life and just come and be with people and really accept them at their level and don't expect great reforms. I think this is where the church went wrong, thinking that the state was going to be different when en masse Christianity came. That it really was going to make a difference if we told people they were going to hell if they didn't go to church.

Admittedly I learned a lot from the flophouse. First we were hassled by police and business types. The city closed us down once. But then we became everybody's darling. We could get everything —but people's time. People came to liturgy and said nice things, but they didn't hang around long enough to do the laundry. The liturgy was real showtime, but the toilet was always running over.

I was never romantic about the guests—transients mostly, psychopaths perhaps, unstable, incapable of keeping a job the day after you found them one. No amount of talking would patch up their lives and certainly getting them a job wouldn't. But it suddenly occurred to me that some of those men were much more sensible about life than I was—with my work ethic, my do-gooder, need-to-achieve, and prove-myself attitudes.

Also, I began to question our right to beg from others, make them uncomfortable, when we had things in our personal lives the people we begged from didn't have. I belonged to the Society of the Precious Blood, a corporation with huge possessions and investments, which would take care of all my food, clothing, medicine, etc. Who was I to make demands of people I was not living up to myself? I thought seriously about leaving my order of priests, but who in hell would want to subject himself to a bishop? And under present structures, there is no other way to function legitimately as a Roman Catholic priest! Besides, being a street priest would have been a big game. A poor person is poor because he has no escape. That is what makes him poor. Dorothy Day once said the only place she could really be poor was in jail. But even there she had a mind and a reason for being there. Jim Groppi became a nigger—no one wanted him around. No priest in the present setup, with any education, can really be poor.

But somehow, if Christianity means anything, it means that we must love people nobody else wants around. And generally, Catholics—Christians—are just as hateful as anyone else.

I gave a talk to priests once and said, "Let's face it, the magic white wafer isn't working." It really doesn't turn people into Christians. They receive Communion every day and still go out and screw their brother. Kill to save a car and justify it!

The Gospel is so simple, fantastically simple and beautiful, and it works. It's the Good Samaritan thing. If there's a guy lying there beat up or in rags, you don't ask why. And that isn't easy. We have to have an honest faith that there is going to be a certain amount of pain and suffering in this life. It makes me angry at a God who set it up this way. He could have done a hell of a lot better. But it's true, and either we face it or face nothing but pain and suffering and none of the joys of life.

A little while back I was giving a talk in Fort Wayne, Indiana, and one of the ladies just looked at me and said, "Father, please go away and rest someplace." What I have to do now is get my life together; I am so fragmented. I'm in a car and I don't even know where I'm going sometimes. I help run Harbor House, the Olé School, which teaches English to the Spanish-speaking. I produce and direct a weekly television program, teach a full college load, write a weekly column, counsel dozens of kids and adults, edit a magazine.

I'm really trying to sort things out. To figure out why I'm here and if I should be. There's no question I'm a heretic in a number of ways. The *Sunday Visitor* reminds me every so often that the only difference between the heretics of the past and the heretics of the present is that the heretics of the present stay in and think they're part of the church. I must have some kind of disease, but I have not given up what I call ministry. I think I am a good celebrator, a good liturgician. It's crazy but I think I am a priest. But I've given up on the church, and certainly have rejected the Roman Catholic Church. And I know the more I condemn it the more you know I love something about it. But it's a monster, and Dan Berrigan has said we have to tear the monster down. I can remember Monsignor John Egan saying, "I'm just going to be around to kick the shit out of it." And that's not being vicious; that's being prophetic, that's being Gospel.

I know that I verge on total bitterness, a total souring about the church. But I also know there is nothing sicker than a priest who leaves in bitterness. If I were to leave in bitterness directed toward a bishop I'd be leaving because of a man who was conned, just like I was conned. I'd leave because of a man living outside his time who can't see beyond the hem of his robe. I look at Pope Paul and I just cry. I think of what he could do if he would really speak out for the poor and oppressed. But who cares about Paul or the bishops? How do *I* respond to the invitation of the Gospel? Some priests and nuns have "left" the institutional church in order to be more Gospel. What are they doing now? I truly don't know. So I live on as a charlatan for the church, a sham, an accomplice to a continuing crime against humanity.

All I can say with any clarity is that the church is dead and the Gospel is alive and I'm half death and half life. Which will win out? I know if I left I wouldn't ask for Rome's permission. It is that authority over my life I protest! I would split the scene completely. People constantly bug me: You still in? Thought you'd be gone years ago. And as much as I talk against the church, it is precisely because I cared about the church and people that I became a priest. I didn't have any romantic notions about it. It wasn't a superficial thing, so leaving it would be that much more painful. Obviously I'm a fighter, but right now I feel so tired, so damned tired.

Representing the church kills me. Wearing the collar kills me. "Oh, you're one of those guys." That's the most painful thing. And as a priest I get up in the pulpit and tell people how to live and be happy when most of the priests I know are miserable. Thousands of priests have left the institutional church, and that church could have kept most of them if she had been human. Nowhere are women more discriminated against than in the church. Like the Scribes and Pharisees, the church continues to lay burdens on people and to increase their guilt. Everlasting hellfire for missing Mass on Sunday! Masturbation is a mortal sin! Birth control turns people into animals, says Pope Paul. A dirty thought deserves hell. Marriage laws made by men who can't think of sex without feeling guilty. Marriage laws! I know a couple who have been married for thirty-five years and who are devout people and who, because of some fluke in the marriage laws, can't be married in the church because they can't take the time and money to pursue their case in canonical courts. This woman attends Mass every Sunday, has for thirty-five years, without receiving Communion. Don Ranly with his Roman collar represents the church that allows that to remain. It makes me want to rip down churches and bomb the Vatican. But why get excited? Most priests grin and say no one really believes that stuff anyway.

There's no sane way to talk about the church, so why talk about it? "You gotta have faith!"

What has kept me going these past four years here is that I don't have people telling me what I can do or not do in my life. With almost any kind of sanctions, I'd just have to pack up. But I don't see any immediate reason for leaving. I don't want to make a hundred thousand a year. But nobody's offered me a hundred thou, and maybe if they did I would be gone tomorrow. It's easy for me to be idealistic, to say what I don't want when I haven't really had the chance for it.

All I know for now is I love this little shack I live in, love my teaching, hate the church, and I better have something or someone damn good to go to if I'm going to leave.

Father Francis Eschweiler

During one week in 1909 diphtheria struck down three of the Eschweiler children. A fourth wavered, the baby Francis. Then he slowly began to recover and in the midst of grief there were prayers of thanksgiving that he had been delivered. Francis grew to be a spindly child who easily tired in the childhood games that were played in the cornfields near his home in a working-class area on Milwaukee's northwest side.

The Eschweilers were a family prone to going to Mass and frequently receiving Holy Communion, so much so that the nuns would often cluck their tongues at this family presumptuous enough to believe they were that worthy.

In a family that eventually produced two other priests and two nuns, it was not surprising that Francis wanted to study for the priesthood. For many the seminary in 1924 was considered a vehicle—to the priesthood, and to social status for those who came out of huge working-class families. As Francis studied to be a priest, the talk around the seminary was divided between God and mammon, the latter getting more interest as men approached ordination. Who would get the wealthy parishes with the generous Mass stipends that would provide a monthly bonus exceeding monthly pay? Who would go to the influential monsignor's parish and begin the climb into church hierarchy and administration?

Francis sounded a sour note in the choir of voices raised up to status, money, power. He wasn't a model seminarian, often late for Rosary or Mass. His grades were among the best, but his awareness of the world outside was off key. Francis could not forget the working-class people. Yet his classmates clamored to serve the men in starched white collars and the women whose hands were not red and roughened like those of his mother and her friends in his old neighborhood.

Avoiding the cultic high-priest role from the start, Father Francis Eschweiler began to form small discussion groups in his first parish, trying to translate to the common man the church's little-used but strong historical background of a social action philosophy. As he was moved from parish to parish—often at the request of fellow priests—he grew stronger in his belief that the Catholic lay person had to be helped not only in spiritual but in temporal matters. He worked with labor organizers and leaders and was branded a socialist for advocating such outlandish acts as a minimum wage law. When his affiliation with union men became too much for the church to bear he was banished to a rural parish where he reached the bleakest moments of his priestly life.

In 1957, at the age of forty-eight, when he was allowed to start a church in a developing suburban area, he sensed that even more drastic changes were coming to Catholicism and that new kinds of structures were going to be required. He had no bylaws to conform to, so he and the people of the Good Shepherd Congregation created their own traditions. The old stipend system was thrown out and creative liturgy introduced. Small groups proliferated. A simple but utilitarian building was constructed that foreshadowed the changes in worship that Vatican II would foster.

Today Fran, or Frannie as everybody calls him, is sixty-four years old. He wears plaid sports jackets and deep-colored shirts and re-

sembles a science teacher more than a priest. When in his car, the cassette player is plugged in and the words of a theologian or philosopher fill the air. He jogs a nine-minute mile five times a week; he swims in cold Wisconsin lakes; he dreads the thought of retirement. Thirty-eight years a priest, and his message has essentially not changed.

A parish of Europeans—Hungarians, Austrians, Slavs—at the height of the Depression. Yes, Milwaukee's St. Michael's was a parish of very poor people. Men were out of work, families hungry; it was a time of discontent in America. People were wondering how everything could have gone so wrong. And so was I. And where was the church while all this went on? In the seminary, when I heard about social action from men like Monsignors Francis Haas and John Ryan, it always appeared to me that that was what priests ought to be doing. All this business of just putting oil and water over people and saying certain words, of limiting ministry exclusively to ritual never had much meaning for me.

As the new priest at St. Michael's I was given church groups like sodalities and the Holy Name Society, and from the beginning I was inclined to put little emphasis on social events and more on social action. In those days social action was outlined pretty nicely in the encyclicals *Rerum Novarum* and *Quadragesimo Anno,* and I'd try to explain these to the men. The radicals and Communists were going at them pretty heavy and these men were ready to listen. Many lived in shacks and they were ready to jump onto anything that promised a better way of life.

I talked about the dignity of man and how his personhood was being violated, that he had no voice in the government of his life, no voice in industry. We had political democracy and freedom, but the workingman had not established his economic democracy. I told the men they would never get their dignity unless they were organized, because the other side was organized against them and if they had to slug it out in the competitive jungle they had better be at least at equal strength.

Although those two social action encyclicals were the pride of the church, too few people talked about them and too few of the church members knew about them. I think a lot of people were surprised that a priest could have any sensitivity toward the day-to-day plight of the workingman. We were supposed to be involved with higher things, things of the spirit.

My pastor at St. Michael's saw enough poverty around, so while he wasn't really enthusiastic about what I was doing he didn't try to stop me. But there were rumors that I was a Commie or a socialist, a rabble rouser. The men I lived with in the rectory felt that the priority in the priest's job was to expand the church sodalities, get the numbers. I believed in small groups, study clubs or discussion groups and that type of thing. I was eased out of St. Michael's because of those differences in philosophy. Plurality wasn't a word we had even heard about in those days.

By today's standards my views are common, accepted. Back in 1937, when I said that the Mass is not a prayer, it is an action, they thought I was a heretic. I always said it was a proclamation of what we believed in and tried to live out, not some isolated rite. Hell, they thought this Fran guy was really off his rocker.

I was an assistant in three places, but I can't say my ministry changed that much during those moves. I learned a lot, but my view was pretty clear-cut: the workingman needed help and I could give it, I felt. I conducted what was known in those days as "labor schools." I went to the blue-collar workers and taught them what to expect when they were part of a bargaining committee and how to handle themselves. I'd work with guys who were organizing and developing unions and just try to give them the Christian ammunition, the basis of good Catholic action as enunciated by the two encyclicals. It was all there: when private initiative fails to meet the needs of people for the common good, it is the right and even the duty of the government to intervene. That would justify minimum wage laws and the Wagner Act, which the big companies hooted were vestiges of socialism. Too often the church was just as vested an interest, and they weren't at the forefront of workers' rights. Somehow the church didn't trust the little man to do or set anything right; somehow he needed some greater authority to dictate to him.

I'm a fighter by nature, but I wear big padded gloves. I never really felt enraged by the priests who stayed in their rectories answering the door and telephone in a kind of "fire station" operation. They didn't want to get their fingernails dirty, but I didn't mind. I just thought that I, this priest, had to do what I could do to get people where they were and relate to them where their greatest needs and problems were. Right then they needed jobs and a decent standard of living. I thought that Christ would never be visible to them unless a priest would really be the kind of man who would show compassion and understanding for their problems and not just gloss everything over with a plenary indulgence.

The workers liked me, I liked them. Down at the chancery they weren't that impressed. From the 1930s and through the big strike of Allis-Chalmers in 1947 there was a string of notes. "Frank, you were quoted as saying thus and so. Lay off." The Allis-Chalmers strike really got me in hot water because so many of the guys who were on the bargaining committee came to me for advice and the people downtown knew about it.

Joe Dombeck was in charge of the picket line and late one night he came to my room, and he was worried. "Going to have violence, Father," he said. "The guys are pretty itchy. They want to go into the plant and take over the machines. They are pressuring me to be violent and if I don't yield they're going someplace else for a leader."

I kept talking to Joe, trying to show him that nonviolence was the right way, and the best way in the long run. I ate beans with the men on the picket line, and I got a chance to reason with them. There was some violence, but we averted a break-in which could have really been a bloodbath.

Then it got back to the chancery that I had attended a UAW meeting and was talking to the stewards. They hit me with the fact that I hadn't gotten permission. Permission to attend a union meeting? At that time I was in the middle of a teaching year at St. Francis Seminary and suddenly I was yanked out. There was an opening and I guess I was positively the only man for the job. What it boiled down to was exile; they exiled me to a little country parish in Kewaskum, forty miles from Milwaukee. It could have been four hundred.

What sunk in and really hurt was that the church obviously was standing on the side of management and didn't want one of their boys mingling with labor types. The big money came from industry; it didn't come from the workingman. The bishop never openly confronted me about my union activities; it all came to me secondhand. But really, I was a marked man and the bigwigs wanted me out of town.

I certainly was somewhat bitter about it, but not that bitter. The bitterness was more of a surface thing. It wasn't a deep-down bitterness that made me want to hate the whole church. I said, Well, that's one dupe who doesn't know. That's not the church. But I was crushed. Plurality wasn't really a word then; neither was relevance. But that's what I was after. For me, as a minister of God, my teaching and living had to make sense to the society around me. This wasn't the Middle Ages; we couldn't just pray and think everything was going to be all right.

And they really knew how to make a guy hurt. Kewaskum wasn't just geographically removed, it was intellectually removed and culturally barren. Good honest farmers who toiled from sunup and then understandably fell asleep at meetings. Good people, but inbred and gossipy as hell. They were quite interrelated. If you stepped on one toe you hit the whole parish.

This was in the early 1950s and I tried to make the best of it. I started a dialogue Mass, but the people had a lot of trouble going with anything different from what they'd done for the past thirty years. Just simple responses in Latin and English and it made them very uncomfortable, but I wanted them to be part of the Mass. I went out on the hay wagons and threshing crews; I ate out in the fields with them. I had a few who were very loyal and whom I could work with and who were willing to be led and to develop during those years.

But those years were full of darkness and frustration. I felt like "God, my God, why have You forsaken me?" I don't want to be dramatic about it, but I had read St. John of the Cross and I felt maybe this was my "dark night." Who knows what I would have done if that had been fifteen years later when leaving the priesthood got to be an accepted thing. Many times I said the hell with this whole thing, with this wall of oppression. But I just couldn't leave the priesthood even though I felt so stymied right then. I was either stubborn, or a hardy believer!

In the years before, I was called a Commie and a socialist. In the years to follow I'd be hated for stands on open housing, I'd be condemned by the church for opposing an encyclical, but when a person feels boxed in, useless, that's the worst hurt of all. There's no way to fight back. And church officials know that, know how to take the fuse out. I can't underestimate the intellectual dryness. Being pulled out of social activism and the excitement of the kids in the seminary and thrown out into the country where nobody read, where current events were grain prices and inches of rainfall.

Cardinal Meyer came into office and he was a more discerning man. When a couple of people in Kewaskum wrote to say this guy Eschweiler was trying to start all that new stuff out there, Meyer took that to be a good sign. He knew me from the seminary and knew I had some abilities, so he transferred me to a little better rural parish for three years. Then he called me in to ask if I'd like to be pastor of a church that didn't yet exist.

Menomonee Falls was really starting to build in 1957, and there was an obvious need for a church. I had always been damned for not keeping traditions, I figured here was the ideal opportunity to start some new traditions. Right from the start I wanted an involved kind of laity. From work in the labor movement, work in the Christian Family Movement since its inception, I saw what the so-called common man could do and how the church often passed him by as incompetent. The layman was the church and he ought to be its voice, be helped to articulate what it stood for. No priest can do that as effectively as a truly motivated layman.

We had an alfalfa field, a couple of sheds and shacks, and an old farmhouse when the diocese turned my parish over to me. The farmhouse was a stinking mess—they had had animals living in there—but we got it cleaned up and that was my home for a while. The public school wouldn't let us use their gym or facilities for services, but the theater owner said we could use the movie house on Sunday mornings. I remember one Sunday morning as I drove in for Mass, the marquee said *The Dangerous Hour*. It was good in there because it was looser, friendly, not so churchy. We had to set up the portable altar and things on the stage every week, and the guys helped out and it created the right atmosphere for the kind of church I wanted.

From the start I had an idea that Good Shepherd should not be the typical church-school combination; there were sure signs that those days were going to be over soon. I wanted more of a community, a center, a "congregation." We had lower-middle-class people who were just hanging on financially, but when the vote came up they were almost unanimous for having a school. There was time before we started building and moved in, so I took time to visit every family. It was a sort of consciousness-raising effort, to free them of the old religious views so that they could grow in a church that was going to have its own style, a relevant kind of celebration —not just hocus-pocus things in liturgy—and ministry.

As with anything new, there were moments of great doubt. The people didn't know where I was trying to lead them. Half the time I wasn't sure either. But I've never had any difficulty talking to God, and I got a lot of reinforcement from the Scripture—seeing Jesus constantly reflecting, going to the desert, bubbling up to the Father. I'd just try to share with God the experience, whether it was joyful, one of great doubt or hesitance, or one that demanded new courage. I prayed for revelation, guidance, things God concealed from the wise and revealed to the little ones. Sometimes I'd just sit in church or in my room and say, "God, what should I do?" And I could come away refreshed . . . and sometimes with an insight into what I should do.

I was a little old (forty-eight) to be starting a parish, but I had seen what worked and what didn't and I was ready for the challenge. On the organization side I forged ahead, starting two Christian Family Movement groups, leadership training for laymen, and working with lay people who helped in the services. But I cooled it at the beginning with my sermons. I had my fingers burned before for saying too much, and perhaps too soon, from the pulpit. I knew my audience was not inclined my way; they were primarily Republican and on the conservative side, but it's hard to keep your ideals hidden long. I remember one Sunday I let out the stops and said something about the public ownership of certain utilities and why should we have all kinds of milk wagons and trucks running down the same street, competing and wasting. Everybody's got to drink milk or use the telephone or have electricity. They started wondering if they didn't have a socialist in their midst.

So many people have said the real place for the church is in the slums. There's no doubt that's more dramatic, that the need there is more pressing, but the new wave of suburbanites had to have the Gospel too. I don't mean pabulum. I mean the fullness of the Gospel. So when open housing became an issue I really pushed our people to come out for it. To say our doors were open to anyone. The resistance was strong, but there were a lot of people who had seen the light and they helped balance those who kept saying, He's bringing them in, he's bringing them in.

One CFM group took up open housing and using the CFM technique—which is actually St. Thomas's prudence bit—they did the three things: observe, judge, and act. They looked over the situation, got the facts, talked to people, then faced themselves with: Is this human or right or good or bad, and then what do we do about it? They found that attitudes were so hardened that the best action they could come up with was to bring in a panel of blacks from an inner city parish who were going around and presenting the housing problems from the black man's point of view.

That meeting was considered by all of us to be a pretty moderate action, but it was a turning point for me in Menomonee Falls. The panel barely got started when a group of John Birchers got up and started screaming. They wanted to confront these people right then. The chairman told them the panel would have their dialogue first and then we'd break into smaller groups for questions. Hell, some of these people hadn't ever talked to a black person. The CFM group had found hardened racism and prejudice and a lot of stupidity. White people didn't think blacks ate like them. It was weird the ideas they had.

The meeting went to the verge of being a violent thing. There was shouting and pushing and shoving, and that all got to the chancery. Then the rumors began to fly. I was trying to bring black people out there to live, and that would reduce property values. I had taken parish money and bought property across the street for low-cost apartments to bring in the blacks. A number of families left to join other parishes. Some thought I was imprudent and tactless. Good pastors are real diplomats and don't lose parishioners. Why did I always have to stir the waters? And be a troublemaker? The chancery reminded me of the departing parishioners, of the "trouble" I was causing in "River City." But through all that I felt tranquil. If I was in trouble for this, I thought, so be it!

There were enough people on my side who saw what I was trying to do, and the numbers of people who came to us kept growing. Parish boundaries didn't mean anything any more and the people who came came because our church offered something different. In fact we have more than two hundred families from the metropolitan Milwaukee area who are now members. There's a joke around that there's a Roman Catholic church, a Catholic church, and a Christian church, and people can take their choice. We're the Christian church.

Vatican II put an emphasis on collegiality, the principle of the layman and the clergy working together, sharing authority, each having a voice and neither controlling the other. There was collegiality in our church from the start. Lay people were given responsibility, they were readers in the liturgy, we had singing at Mass and dialogue Mass. And a really important point: Our laymen began to see their religious belief not just as something they expressed in church but which had to be taken into the community, into their daily lives.

I wouldn't say I flaunted doing things in those days that were not approved. Let's put it this way: I went as far as I possibly could under the restrictions and perhaps once in a while I leaned on the restrictions too hard for what I believed was the good of the church. So when Vatican II came along, it wasn't like a floodgate of new things being opened to us. Vatican II just validated a lot of things we were doing all along.

I was in my fifties when Vatican II occurred, and most priests my age were threatened by it, fought it. Our training had never demanded that we update, never really demanded we re-evaluate things and chart new courses. Then Vatican II required new and developing theology, new thinking, and many of the men my age weren't capable of coping with the challenge to change. They were threatened by the thought of laymen taking over positions of power and even handling the money, which, next to the host, was to them the most sacred thing. I felt that my role was secure, because while the power of the priest was now a thing to be shared —the exercise of power was never "my thing" anyway—nevertheless people still needed the "Word" and we didn't have too many people around trained to give the Word.

Vatican II just seemed to make life a lot easier for me. Looking back, I can call the last ten years of my ministry the most exhilarating. About five years ago I dropped Confession before First Communion and was very careful to validate my position from the pulpit. That's common practice now, but then it was something. Psychologically it didn't make sense to pretend to have a child seven years old relating to God on that kind of a profound level. Sin involves a relationship with God and neighbor, either cooling it or breaking it, and I just didn't feel children of that age were mature enough to enter that kind of relationship with anybody; and they certainly weren't capable of walking out on God or even consciously offending Him.

There were some calls to the chancery and the chancery told me I had to take back what I said. I asked why, and I was told there was some directive on it. I said I knew of no law about compulsory Confession for children and I'd done some reading on the history of Confession and I didn't see the need for it at that age. I told them the official church could always find a directive someplace to cover any instance of anything and that I wasn't going to change. They never pushed me on the point again. I think priests quit too easily sometimes. All you have to do is lean on the door and it opens.

I really tried not to duck issues as they came up in my ministry—

from open housing to Confession. I didn't always do right, but I did something. And for an old clerical codger, I was questioned now and then by the media about the church's stance on this or that. When *Humanae Vitae* came out and I opposed it in favor of personal conscience in reference to a responsible use of contraception in marriage, a television reporter did an interview in my living room and really gave me a loaded question. It went something like "Father Eschweiler, it's known that you've taken a position that people have the freedom to form their own conscience regarding birth control. How is it that other priests haven't taken that stand?"

The camera was running; I didn't have time to think. So I did say, "I can't speak for other priests, but maybe they haven't done the necessary reading that a priest ought to be doing to keep current on a subject like this. And some of the best theologians—with all due respect to the Pope—have said that we need to respect the consciences of responsible people in this matter, that it is our pastoral duty to provide them with moral guidelines that will help them to a right conscience in this matter of family limitation." I said, "Vatican II clearly equated the importance of conjugal love along with the procreative purpose of marriage, and how are you able to sustain that if you have no option except the precarious practice of rhythm or simply total abstinence if you concluded that having more children would be irresponsible in your case?"

Personal conscience wasn't a new issue, I maintained. Vatican II had clearly stated that parents alone had to make the decision about how many children they should have in view of their economic situation, the physical and mental health of the mother, even the total good of the community. As I became more aware of what was really involved in bearing and raising children, as I listened to parents grappling with this problem, my views changed through the years until I got to the point where I made no yes or no judgment on contraceptives. I gave couples the guidelines and asked them to make up their minds. I told them that I felt there were people who in given instances certainly were morally permitted to prevent conception unnaturally, but that each couple had to come to grips with their own conscience in this matter and come to a personal Christian decision about what would constitute responsible parenthood in their situation.

I knew it would be only a matter of time for some kind of reaction from the chancery after the interview. "Dear Frank: Don't put us priests all in the same category. We're not all that stupid and it's imprudent of you to try and speak for the church and diocese. This is the official position of the church and how can you differ with that?" So the chancery says all priests aren't stupid—and I know that—but then they fall back on doctrine for a rebuttal.

So I wrote back. The fellow who had to write on behalf of the chancery is really a good boy; I had him in seminary. I said that I didn't mean to impugn all the clergy or their intelligence but I felt many hadn't done their homework, so they didn't know there were any options other than the old hard line. And I said Pope Paul had kind of retracted what Vatican II had gone forward with in the vision of what marriage ought to be.

There were the usual hate letters too, most of them unsigned and irrational. But the letter that hurt the most was from the pastor of my parish where I went to school and celebrated my first Mass. "*Sentire cum Ecclesia*," he said, "think and feel with the church, Frank." It's an old expression we used in the seminary. If you thought and felt with the church and were an obedient son, that was the ultimate. And then he resorted to a familiar, sentimental, and hackneyed cliché: "Your dear mother would be upset in her grave if she knew."

When you're younger you wonder if you aren't crazy sometimes because you're out there alone. And when you're older you still question your sanity. Maybe I'm tactless, because I am always getting in trouble. I had my faculties taken away once when I was confessor to sisters in a convent. I was doing some counseling and the mother superior wrote the bishop that this man was unsettling the community with his conferences. And the nuns were running over to his room for "counseling." If I was to do it over again I wouldn't have spent so much time with some of those nuns. What I mean is, many of them were more sick than sinning. Maybe I was imprudent, but at any rate my intentions were honest. What they wanted was a friend mostly. That was a bad word too—"friend"—because PF's, i.e., "particular friendships," in those days were taboo. Even worse, they told the superior I helped them. But again, how to come to grips with a woman who is frustrated, unhappy about her life? Turn her out with two Hail Marys, or try to make some sense out of her life, tie it in to what the Gospel is telling each of us. The prevailing and accepted practice at that time would turn her out with two Hail Marys and not get "involved." The curt letter followed from the chancery: "Your faculties for hearing Sisters' Confessions are hereby suspended." No explanation. That's oppressive, that's stifling, and it hurts. And you say to yourself many times that you've had it. But for me it always seemed like things opened up. That new opportunities presented themselves if I had the patience to stick around. I think many of the men who have left gave up too quickly. They weren't willing to wait and lean on the door, wait some more and lean some more. I found it works. The door keeps opening further and further.

When I look back to see what really kept me in and functioning I always end up saying "people." Lay groups like the Christian Family Movement—and I've been in that for twenty-seven years—gave me the feeling that I was getting through. Given the opportunity, the Spirit could really work in these groups, transform these people. Five or six couples and I sitting around in a CFM group, in a home, exploring our faith, trying to find out what God is summoning us to do in one facet of our lives. Maybe we'd take a problem like race relations and after carefully observing and judging on the matter the people would realize they really couldn't go on calling themselves Christians and still harbor these hatreds, and they had to do something positive about it. Or in their marriages, they had to start really loving or caring for that person right next to them. CFM helped me to save my own soul and my priesthood, really. Without some tangible evidence that what I stood for and talked about was being understood and incorporated in a few lives I never could have gone on. While I was nourishing them with the Word which gives life, they were giving me hope.

This is the church, these people, and this is worth working for, and struggling for as a priest, not PRIEST. I feel that this is the people business at the highest, deepest, most profound level. Where men and God meet, and I'm the coordinator of that. I help create a condition whereby the two can come together, where people can experience the "Good News" and realize the fullness of God, where they can come to the Father by coming into contact with the humanity of Jesus.

I can't think of any other place where I could be as effective in reaching these people at such a level. I don't regard my commitment to the formal church as something mandatory simply because of my vows. Vows after all will never hold a man together when the ground from under gives way. It's something else that is instinctive, something so deeply embedded in my faith, so firmly rooted in the core of my person, that somehow the Spirit calls me to work this way, even with a structure that too often is immobile, intransigent, and impervious to any kind of change. I'd like to think with St. Paul that it is the "love of Christ" that "drives me on."

A word about institutions. I feel with Gregory Baum that all institutions—whether it's the Catholic Church, General Motors, the National Association of Manufacturers, or the government with its bureaucracies—have built-in "pathologies" which make them turn in on themselves and by gradual erosion turn away from the purposes for which they were originally established. Once "established," they become blind to the needs and demands of the people they were intended to serve. They become hidebound and insensitive to persons. They become impersonal and defensive as they become big. The "bigger" and more powerful they get, the more they turn their energies to self-preservation of the institution rather than to the service of persons. It is a kind of institutional sickness which plagues them and makes them paralytic, unable to "move." Any suggestions for change are put down as dangerous, subversive, and destructive of that sacred cow which we call "law and order."

But for all their flaws and weaknesses, institutions are not only here to stay, they are necessary and viable structures within which men are called to grow and work. We cannot live without them. Since they are always in need of reform it is imperative that people with charisma or leadership dynamics stay in to bring about the necessary evolution of change and reform from within—to keep the institution honest and human and sensitive to its true purposes. And in this way ultimately create a new institution.

The only alternative I see to this is to jump over the wall—to drop out. Maybe we need a few people to do this—to witness to the corruption of the existing establishment, to point up the need for radical change. But to cop out is generally to be alone, alienated, on one's own. I for one can't work out there alone, by myself. To me the church, the priesthood, is still the frame of reference I need to work from. I'll bypass the rigamarole, the excess baggage, the needless paraphernalia which the simple structure that Jesus instituted did not include. Frankly, I have a quarrel with some of the priests who have decided to drop out and, I believe, who have quit too soon. Many of them were precisely the kind of charismatic men who abandoned the "sinking ship" when they were most needed. And some of them, it seems to me, have been less than honest in stating upon their leaving that they were embarking upon some new and more productive "ministry out there"—free from the inhibiting and stifling roadblocks that the institutional church put in their way. I just haven't seen any significant, exciting new ministries that have emerged in the promised land out there. Mostly they are married, and I have no quarrel with that call if that's what it is, and maybe that's "ministry" enough for them. But let's not call it by another name.

I feel bad about the many good young men who have left, and I wish them the best. Some of them who have worked with me have helped to free me. I wish they had seen fit to bypass the peripheral elements within the structure while remaining faithful to the substance of the church.

I still think the priest has great power. I think he can have a persuasive influence—in the right sense, not manipulating people, not swarming all over them—and lead them to freedom. There are such great opportunities to completely free people from their inadequacies, fears, hangups, and bring out the best potential. Like Jesus did, a priest can draw people out.

And I'm not trying to make a case for those priests who just stay in, many of whom are already dead but just not yet buried. I make a plea for men to stay in creatively, who will be true to themselves, moving as their conscience tells them to move, and being responsive to the Spirit. We stifle the Spirit every day, all of us do, because we get our knuckles rapped. If enough people believe in change and improving the quality of life in the Church, the structure will change in due time. We found that out here at Good Shepherd.

I try to keep my eyes on Jesus. He was so strong, and yet so human. He always kept on coming, and yet he needed help, and asked for it. Not only from his Father, but from his friends. "Sit down here and watch with me," he pleaded. "My soul is sad unto death." I would hope that priests generally, and young priests in particular, would ponder deeply these words in the Transfiguration account in Mark's gospel: ". . . looking around they no longer saw anyone with them—only Jesus." A priest will keep a right perspective by fixing his eyes on Jesus. He is our "Way." Also our "Way out" of frustration and despair. No doubt optional celibacy is important and will open new doors for many to find fulfillment in their ministry. But I have a nagging feeling that the "marriage thing," which is quite a demanding ministry by itself, will not free the priest for all the kinds of fulfillment that he is really looking for—nor from the impediments, hangups, and frustrations that establishments impose. Like all people, the priest needs to be loved and he wants to succeed. And all of us, priests and lay people, must find all kinds of ways to give him the love that humanly he needs and help him to reach that measure of success in his ministry that he must have if he is to experience a sense of fulfillment and well-being as a person and a priest. Let's face it, lack of success can be a priest's problem, unless his faith is deep and he doesn't expect too much tangible evidence of success. The parable of the seed says a lot to me. Most of it fell on ground that wouldn't receive it. What the hell success did Jesus have? Twelve guys he spent three years on, and they weren't that solidly faithful. We priests are human and we have to see some signs that some seeds are taking root. I admit to my own lack of faith in this regard, always wanting things to germinate overnight. I think we should wait a "week"! But if you are true to yourself you really can't lose. You may look like a loser for ten or more years, but ultimately the day of vindication comes.

I am staying around—and have stayed around—because I'm tenacious, but also I'm a hopeful man. If I abandon the ship, then a lot of others will take over the wheel, and places like Good Shepherd might not be. We are an island here, an option, a center. We are not a geographical parish. We serve hundreds of people from all over the area who are drawn here because they find something that is credible, that makes sense. We need a multiplication of different kinds of islands today to meet the varied needs of people, not just mimeographed parishes all doing the same thing. While we hang in here and stay on deck—where "the Spirit breathes where He will" and manifests Himself in a variety of styles of ministry and worship—we at Good Shepherd are proud to be, to quote a few phrases from our "Parish Philosophy,"

A happening that is
always happening,
where the Word goes out
that God is Love
and all is well . . .
A CONGREGATION *of people*
who gather and sing
because they believe the news
is good . . .
where there is always a meal
at which to drink "new wine"
. . . where reconciliation and forgiveness
are always a CELEBRATION.

We are proud to serve the church at large by being responsibly different as we respond to the Spirit in being

a fellowship of believers
who seek always to be open to
and listening to the Spirit
as He speaks to us
and summons us
to see new visions,
to chart new courses,
and to accept new challenges
which enable us to grow.
and develop
and become whole.

At least we've done something "to make all things new," and it's been exciting, serving people who want and need more than carbon copy ministry—and it's been worth staying in for.

I'm hopeful. Last week we had a meeting of thirty interested priests who work together to create good liturgy. I helped start the group, and those men by their attendance and interest give me hope. And we give hope to one another. And they'll push out in new directions and they're not going to be stymied or hampered. And that courage reinforces an old hand like me to stay around for a while.

Bishop Thomas Gumbleton

In a corner room of the Sacred Heart rectory in Detroit it is not yet six o'clock and a priest is pulling the chenille bedspread over his sagging mattress. He has a tranquil, almost bland, look on his face in the midst of a variety of assaults. The early morning traffic screams by on Interstate 95, which knifes through the parish. The vacant lot behind the church shows only a few scrubs of grass, but mostly dingy Styrofoam cups and broken whiskey, wine, and beer bottles. A stale, sour odor comes through the window. Even the chenille bedspread assaults, leaving tiny pills of white on his black suit.

He enters his office ten minutes later and takes out a book many priests his age—forty-three—have abandoned: the breviary. He says his morning prayers and then, while munching on doughnuts staled by a day in his desk, he finishes reading a book on theology. The phone will start ringing soon. He brushes crumbs off the desk and glances at the calendar. He will attend many meetings, teach a class in "The Church's Ministry to the Poor," and visit with a parish council that has asked him to help them get started. His day will be busy, taken up with minutiae as well as the massive problems of closing Detroit Catholic schools.

When Thomas Gumbleton was named auxiliary bishop in Detroit in 1968 at the age of thirty-eight, he was the youngest among the three hundred bishops and one of the youngest ever chosen in America. Except for the fact that he was so young, there was nothing particularly distinguishing about this short, slight man with a close-cropped hair style. Yet in the past five years Gumbleton has proved to be somewhat of a Becket, a roiler of waters in the most exclusive American clerical club there is. In his own quiet way and with his simple life style he has called for a reassessment of the role of American hierarchy.

He has marched for the poor in Detroit, with POW families against the war in Washington, backed McGovern and the Berrigans. When he travels to conferences he stays in $5-a-day YMCA rooms and eats in simple restaurants, and while the cocktail parties go on, Gumbleton might be playing an aggressive game of handball at the Y.

His early background is like that of many priests—a poor, large, religious family. The Gumbletons had nine, including a mentally retarded girl who has been institutionalized since she was ten. When Tom came along in 1930, the sixth child, his father was working three jobs—full time at an axle plant, part time as a bookkeeper, and working at home as a notary—in addition to attending night school. In 1932, with his wife and eight children posing with him, he was featured in a Detroit newspaper when he graduated from college.

As a youngster, Tom's life was homey, uncomplicated. Although the Gumbletons had little themselves, they often helped to clothe and feed needier families. And they were people of faith. Tom would often see his father kneeling beside the bed at night reciting his daily Rosary. His mother would feed and dress all the children and get them off to Masses on Sunday, all the while fasting so she could receive Communion at the twelve-thirty.

With a disarming shyness coupled with a Knute Rockne–like

desire to win in sports, he was a well-liked seminarian who earned the best grades in his class throughout his eight years. After parish and chancery assignments he was sent to Rome to study and there he came to an understanding of canon law that he felt the American hierarchy had failed to see.

The Second Vatican Council was over and Gumbleton returned to the Detroit chancery to work, this time to be faced with growing dissatisfaction and defection in the long black line of priests. It caused him to wonder if those who were leaving didn't have a point. Most men have the luxury of months or years of weighing that decision. Tom Gumbleton's decision was forced when a letter arrived from Rome stating that the Holy Father had selected him to be a bishop.

When I was in grade school my view of a priest was a very simple one. The priest was the man at the altar saying Mass, the man who dispensed sacraments and occasionally report cards over at Epiphany School, where I went. It was a very sacramental priesthood and I was drawn to that, drawn to the beauty of the liturgy. I had no idea how a priest would spend the rest of his time when he wasn't in public view.

I can remember in the second or third grade that there were a couple of kids in our house, and I don't know how we got into it, but we were talking about the apostles. I can remember my mother being in the kitchen doing some baking and saying, "Did I hear you say you wanted to become a priest?" What we were saying was "Wouldn't it be neat to be an apostle, someone who could do a really tough job, someone called because he had the stuff to do it."

There was a very vague thing in the back of my mind all through grade school, and then a Passionist came to the school, gave a vocation talk, and handed out a questionnaire. Would you like to be a priest? Would you like to be a Passionist? And the years of thinking but not really agonizing over being called and wanting to follow resulted in my answering, "Yes, I want to be a priest. No, I don't want to be a Passionist." It was the first time I'd ever put it on paper or said it to anybody.

Going right out of grade school and into a seminary can be tough for a kid, but I was fortunate to have some modifying factors. For one thing, I lived at home. My sister was always bringing her friends around, so I went through minor seminary aware that there was an opposite sex and in fact I had liked a girl quite a bit at the end of grade school. But I knew I wanted to be a priest, priests didn't marry, so I didn't date or let our relationship go very far. Also, I was very big on sports, and sports were a big thing in the seminary. I read that a lot of that emphasis is to displace sexuality and maybe that's true, but I loved sports.

I took to the seminary readily. I was fascinated by the place. I would get there an hour early in the morning so I could study and I studied a lot in the evenings at home. I worked hard and I did get very good marks; I guess all A's except for a C my first quarter in algebra and a B in physics. With all of us at home, it wasn't the most ideal place to study, but we all managed and I think my mother realized that it was a healthier thing for me to be in a family setting rather than be in an artificial situation with a bunch of boys boarding at the seminary. I never realized how hard it is for some kids to get through adolescence until I started hearing confessions. I'm not suggesting I had the perfect adolescence; later in my life I had to go through an adjustment on relationships with everybody, especially women, but I did have a chance to develop normal heterosexual friendships, which would never have happened boarding at the seminary.

In college we had a system where men in the third and fourth year were in charge of the student government, and in the fourth year somebody was named head prefect. I was picked for that and I was surprised, because they usually picked a more quiet and scholarly type for the job and I didn't have that kind of reputation. The prefect was looked upon as a sort of a scary figure among the younger students, and the person who was prefect often became very aware of his power, the first power he was ever given to exercise. It's not untypical for people to overreact, to feel that they have to impress people with their power and authority and feel they have to be standoffish, not being too friendly or human because they'll take advantage of you. Then there's the other extreme where the person wants to be buddy-buddy with everybody.

I wanted to just be Tom Gumbleton, just a natural guy, willing to have fun and not be on a pedestal but extremely careful to give a good example by the way I treated people. My classmates would know better than I, but I don't think being prefect made that much difference, I don't think I put on airs. In fact, one class counselor told me that the faculty thought I lacked leadership, that I wasn't one who would stand out and lead. I was the guy who was usually elected secretary or treasurer and I didn't find it easy to be in the role of authority over people.

The seminary years were happy, fruitful, and all of us looked forward to ordination day. If seminarians had any doubts about the priesthood then, they were cast in the light of Were we worthy? That was a scary thing in those days because a bad priest was something we didn't even talk about. The thought of being ordained and then finding you really weren't fit to be a priest was a fear next to death itself. And I prayed very sincerely that if I didn't belong I would discover it and leave.

Ordination day and first Mass came and went without my feeling any special high about them. They were the natural culmination of what I'd studied for; I felt very good, but I was looking to my first real work as a parish priest, which I thought I would probably be doing for the rest of my life. There's a lot of joking that goes on about people graduating from the seminary and starting to plot out their path to becoming a bishop. There really wasn't any of that in our class. The only ones I can remember people really talking about as being potential bishops were a couple of men two years ahead of me, Jamie Kavanaugh and Ed Szoka.* Both were very talented men and in many ways model seminarians.

We went out as priests very much law-and-order men. Later, after I studied canon law, I could say that laws are made for man, not man for laws, but nobody seemed to be saying that in 1956. I still believe that people should not casually disregard liturgical rules or other disciplinary regulations, but the law must never become a straitjacket. A perfect example: The law of the breviary was a law that in a sense said something more fundamental than just a rule about saying particular prayers. Rather, a priest had to be a man of prayer.

We had a man who came into the seminary after serving in World War II and who never really understood Latin. The Latin breviary was a hindrance to prayer for him; he struggled through it and he got nothing from it. People like him should have said a long time ago, I have to pray, but this is hindering me in praying, so I have to do something different. Because above all else I have to be a man of prayer. Latin came easily to me. In the seminary I went through the 150 psalms that are the basis of the breviary, working with a commentary, and I tried to understand them as best I could. The breviary for me is meaningful prayer. The law was never meant to put a burden on people; that's the kind of thing that Jesus talked about when he criticized the Pharisees for putting those unspeakable burdens on the backs of people. So at times you can excuse yourself from the law or in a sense go beyond the word of the law to fulfill the spirit of it. We are supposed to have a feeling for people and that includes ourselves and we shouldn't let the law destroy us.

* Kavanaugh left the priesthood in June 1966 after writing the best-selling *A Modern Priest Looks at His Outdated Church*. Szoka was named bishop of Gaylord, Michigan, in 1971.

The spirit of the law, that's very important, not just doing gymnastics with the law to get around it. This is a rather poor example, but I was with a couple of bishops—this is before I was one—in a motel room and we wanted to celebrate Mass. There is a law, still in the code, that Mass cannot be said in a bedroom. Now this was a bedroom by any definition, but we drew an imaginary line and on one side it became a sitting room and we said Mass there. No malice, but it was doing gymnastics with church laws to fulfill the word rather than the sense of the law.

So, anyway, I was assigned to my first parish. By that time I had saved up enough money and coupled with what I received at ordination I was able to buy a $1,600 Chevy, very conscious that I did not want car payments or other money worries hounding me. We got $75 a month then, but Mass stipends went into a kitty and we got a part of that each month, perhaps another $100. That bothered me from the start although I knew that people want to give something for and in a sense identify with a Mass. But people would come into the rectory saying, "I want to buy a Mass, Father." I'm much more comfortable now that stipend money goes to the parish and the salaries have been upgraded.*

At the parish I taught religion classes in the grade and high schools and I realized that the contact with these young people was one of the most important occupations I had. We started groups like Young Christian Students, and then I got to know the parents through the kids. We started Christian Family Movement groups, and pretty soon I was very busy. Like most parish priests of my day, I was committed to the idea that that parish marked the boundaries of my life. Everything would be for them—teaching, counseling, giving the sacraments, taking care of the sick. I had a day off, and it was good to play ball, go out to eat or to a movie, but the whole thing was that parish.

* The average priest in the Detroit Archdiocese earns $4,500 a year; Gumbleton's salary is $6,000.

I was happy. There was an assistant there—he's died since—who was very influential. He'd been a priest for eighteen years and still was a very giving kind of person, very gentle. He really taught me how to hear confessions and explained that it was a great way to come in contact with people, and it could really be a help to them if the priest took time—maybe just a half minute or so—to show them you cared. Not just saying the absolution and closing the door.

Things went well for me except I think I was a little hard for one of the guys in the rectory to take. He just felt I let people walk all over us. If somebody called in the middle of the night and wanted to know what time Mass was, I would tell them. This didn't bother me; I could fall back to sleep in ten seconds anyhow. This other guy thought that we should teach the parishioners that we had hours, and that if we trained them they wouldn't be calling up all hours of the night. He said I was a damn fool to answer them and he said I should just tell them to call in the morning and hang up. Men moved in and out of the rectory during my four years and I always seemed to get along better with the less structured guys who didn't want to observe office hours and so-called propriety.

After the four years I was called in to be an assistant chancellor, which was a typical job for a young priest but a surprise. I could have seen teaching for some time at the seminary in between parish assignments as a more likely thing for me. Some people think that a job in the chancery is automatically a step up the ladder toward being a bishop. In our diocese it hadn't worked that way and often pastors of big churches or the rector at the seminary would be named when an opening occurred. At that point if a job higher up the line occurred to me it was to be pastor of my own church.

When I got down there I quickly realized that this mystique about the chancery was a lot of—I don't know what to call it. For me there just wasn't much there of any great moment. My job was to read through all the forms that had been filed for mixed marriages in the diocese and to grant dispensations. I had to make sure the form was filled out correctly, signed by the parish priest, and that there was cause for the dispensation and the right dispensation was being asked for and so on.

It was a lot less challenging than anything, really anything that I did in the parish. I could have as easily granted the dispensation in the parish as send the forms downtown. It all seemed very hollow to me, yet there could be the tendency to want to somehow keep up the pretense that you were really doing something big and important, that person was in a position of great authority. I tried to be honest with my friends about the work; it didn't amount to a hill of beans and I was fed up with it. I was frustrated, felt useless and, for the first time as a priest, unhappy.

After a year I was going to ask Archbishop Dearden to send me back to a parish. It was at that time that he asked me if I wanted to go to Rome to study canon law. When your bishop asked in those days he was in a sense assigning, but I really tried to make a decision whether or not I should go. It was a crucial decision because in a way I was then committing myself to life internment at the chancery. But I thought perhaps after two years I'd come back with a different perspective on the job and maybe things would be done in a different way. If not, I would just be resigned to a few years of adjusting, because I couldn't spend the diocese's money for studies abroad and then not do the work. Three things were on my mind: I was fascinated with the chance of studying in Europe; I wanted to escape the present situation; and I was very much in the bag of doing what I was assigned to do. I was thirty-one at the time.

It turned out to be a lot more beneficial than I ever thought and gave me insights that would be helpful when I would be looked to as an authority figure. What I began to see more than anything as I studied in Rome was the humanness of the system that I hadn't been aware of, because I had only seen the American church. Church law had the image of being a rigoristic, legalistic system that binds people in a straitjacket. But I began to see that because church law came from the Roman system of law it had to be used as part of a whole system if it was to be used correctly. In the United States we lived civilly under essentially what was English common law and ecclesiastically under canon or Roman law, and there was a transfer to the detriment of canon law. The kinds of things that would allow the system of canon law some flexibility, that would allow it to be the human sort of system it is, allowing for human weaknesses and frailties, were wiped out in the American application of canon law because those things that allowed for flexibility were not built into the American civil system of law.

Roman law is highly codified, everything is spelled out in precise detail, so it could very quickly become a straitjacket. But built into the law are ways that you can excuse yourself from observing it. For instance, take the church's disciplinary laws like fasting and abstinence or Mass on Sunday. We learned to follow those laws slavishly, but actually within canon law it is expected that there would be times where you wouldn't be able to live up to the letter of the law. If a person ate or drank by accident before going to Communion, he could have excused himself from that law. We would never think, in the American civil system, of saying I need dispensation from this law because circumstances are such that I'm going to find it very hard to obey it.

But church dispensations are part of the church law system. Also there is such a thing as developing a custom contrary to the law, where it becomes clear that the law is not applicable for one reason or another, so the community can act contrary to the law. The custom after a set period of time in fact changes the law.

Also there is the possibility of mitigation of the law in difficult situations. This is not a concept we Americans with our civil law tradition take to very readily. But church law draws on Roman civil law, which considers law an art, "the art of the good and equitable." This "art" finds the way to correct the strict letter of a law which works an injury or which is not in harmony with natural justice. This is known in canon law as the proper use of *equity*. There is also *epikeia*. This is a benign application of law according to what is good and equitable on the basis that the lawmaker does not intend some particular case to be included under his general law because of exceptional circumstances.

I guess one of the things I was discovering was that church law really allows a lot of room to move. It is a system of law that throws real responsibility on the individual person. And this means there is real respect for the person, a real understanding that members of the church are adults and therefore capable of making decisions for themselves. And this enables people to continue to grow.

Right about the time of Vatican II, Pope John XXIII promulgated the decree *Veterum et Sapientiae* that glorified the classical languages and pronounced that Latin was the official language of the church and that seminary courses in philosophy and theology had to be taught in Latin. I was there as Pope John solemnly presented this decree in St. Peter's Basilica, with the cardinals, archbishops, and bishops flocked around, and it was a very impressive sight.

I went back to classes at the Lateran University, which is called the Pope's University, and found the professors still lecturing in Italian just as before and with no thought of changing. Their frame of mind was that maybe we'll get back to Latin, but you can't do it overnight. It may come, but don't get excited about it.

But in the United States there was a big furor. I remember guys writing me in a panic: "The Pope said it and the bishops over here are thinking we have to throw out the English textbooks and start lecturing in Latin again." American professors were going through agonies over the thing. In Rome, nothing. It opened my eyes that not every word from the Pope had to be slavishly adhered to.

After an initial period in Rome of loneliness and feeling very lost I began to get more comfortable and to enjoy the surroundings and the atmosphere. But there were a lot of things I was very uncomfortable with as far as Rome was concerned. It seemed there was a real cleavage between clergy and people over there, a contempt for priests, disdain. The people would see the cardinals driving around in big cars, so out of touch with the common people, and this seemed to spread over into the clergy at large. Those in authority had little touch with the common person. The Curia blocked the Pope from outside contacts, and I began to see this as a serious defect in the whole system. Pope John, I think, tried to break through, still he was always surrounded by his entourage, and he really couldn't. It reminded me of the sort of thing Morris West describes in *The Shoes of the Fisherman,* where the Pope wants to break out of the Vatican regimen and walk around in the streets.

But Vatican II was on and some of the finest theologians of our time came and spoke to us. Rahner, Congar, Küng, John Courtney Murray, Barnabas Ahern. The church seemed to be developing in a really good way, but there was no hint—even those men had no hint—of the radical changes that were to come.

I came back to the chancery in 1964 just hoping that things would be different from what I had left and very quickly they were. Cardinal Dearden had been much involved in the Council and was eager to make it a reality back home. He began to come in more contact with priests and lay people too and he began to see new needs. I got an opportunity to develop a poverty program, getting the diocese involved with OEO and their money. I got into the beginnings of new parishes and the construction and renovation of church buildings, trying to help in designing worship space most effectively for the renewed liturgy.

In 1965 and 1966 the cracks in the dike weren't yet showing, in that great numbers of religious hadn't really left yet, but something was happening and we wanted to get a better picture of what priests' attitudes were, so I got involved in setting up meetings of open discussions between the cardinal and priests of the diocese. The cardinal met with sixty or seventy priests a week for eight weeks and we followed up with a questionnaire. Among the things that came strongly back was that there was a lot of ill feeling about the pastor-assistant relationship. There was the feeling that the rectory was the pastor's home, the housekeeper was the pastor's housekeeper, and the assistants were sort of tolerated. Many had no rights and couldn't even bring their friends in to visit.

We also discovered that many priests were beginning to feel inadequate to the new pastoral demands that were being made of them. So we started a crash course on how to be a pastor for those men about to be named to the position. Also, a lot of older priests felt ill at ease with the new liturgy. Many too were not familiar with any other kind of relationship in the rectory than the old "pastor-assistant" relationship, which often left the assistant pretty much as a non-person. But the system perpetuated itself because many times the assistant who spent his priesthood in that kind of relationship was not able to act any different as a pastor than the men he had worked with previously.

On into the 1960s, the exodus of priests accelerated. If I had been in a parish I probably wouldn't have been that aware of how many men were leaving and why. Because of my work in the chancery I was very much aware of every guy who was going and his reasons. Many left to get married, and the pressure was building for a change in the celibacy laws. This made me start to think about it. Before that I really never gave celibacy a second thought. And then the pressures built up in my own mind and the question formed: Do we really need a law like this? Is it inhumane and an unfair denial of rights, and did people really choose it or not? A number of the guys who were leaving were saying things like "Look, I just didn't know what I was getting into." The first couple of times it happened, I reacted: "How could you not know what you were doing? You were twenty-six years old like everybody else."

As more guys left I had to face myself with the fact that I was one of those people who had never made a serious choice on celibacy. And I realized I didn't have as much foundation for celibacy as I thought I did and that all it amounted to was a discipline that I had accepted without a rationale or very strong explicit motivation for celibacy as such—other than the basic motivation of wanting to be a priest. This is what I wanted, what I felt called to by God, and celibacy was just an accepted part of it.

I wore my collar all the time as a safeguard for my celibacy; that was what I was trained to do. I was trained that celibacy was a good and necessary law, but I came to a point where that wasn't enough any more. Too many people were throwing up challenges to it. Personalism and personal relations were beginning to be stressed in new ministries. Previously we had been taught that such things endangered your work rather than enhanced it. I saw personalism as basically a good movement in the church, where the priest had to say who he was as a person, rather than how well he conformed to a mold.

Another thing that affected me was that I began to know a lot more about what was happening to older priests. Many men had never come to grips with themselves and their sexuality. I mentioned sports as one form of displaced sexuality in the priesthood. I saw that drinking, boats, big cars, and summer cottages were sometimes other forms. So much of this was because the men could not relate to people, and they either drowned themselves with alcohol or related to some safe material thing. I saw what this did to some men after years and years in the priesthood. Complaints would come in on the same people, who had been insensitive at a funeral or short to a person in need. Would I end up like that?

I wondered if I was really committed to celibacy or if I had just accepted it as part of the package and now was finding out I wasn't all that committed. Maybe getting married would be a good idea. Guys I was close to would come and see me and tell me it just wasn't worth it any more and they were leaving. And I knew I just couldn't put all the questions aside.

I had to confront myself with whether I could continue as a priest, whether I wanted to, whether it would be possible to. I'm saying this a lot more explicitly than I think it was happening at the time, but it was constantly in the background of my thinking. I never did reach a point where I came up against it and said, O.K., you have to decide by a certain date. But you can't be in that kind of limbo long. As it turned out, I had to come to terms very quickly.

I received a letter from the Apostolic Delegate and opened it thinking it was a request for a reference on a man the Pope was considering for bishop. Instead it said the Holy Father wanted to make me a bishop. Would I accept? I had no inkling I was even being considered; I had to decide pretty quickly and a lot of things crossed my mind. If I said yes to this, I was saying yes to the idea of being celibate, because if they ever changed the law I was sure they were not going to change it for bishops.

It may sound corny, but after opening that letter the first thing I did was go to church. I just sat up in the balcony for a while and prayed. I prayed that I could honestly make a choice now—at age thirty-eight—about the priesthood. Celibacy was only one thing; I had to be honest with myself as to how committed I really was to the priesthood. And if I said yes to the priesthood I could in honesty say yes to the appointment as bishop.

Laicization was beginning to be granted, so if a priest wanted to opt out the opportunity was there in a way it had never been before. I had not ever really thought of asking for laicization, and yet I had a very clear realization that if I said yes to this call to be a bishop I would not want to do it unless I was firmly and irrevocably committed to the priesthood. It may sound a bit unreal, but actually it wasn't the kind of thing where I said, Gosh, I've always wanted to be a bishop and here's my chance. For me the letter about being a bishop was really an occasion when I thought through in a short time and prayed quite intensely over the basic call to the priesthood. When I walked out of the church I had made a second choice about the priesthood: I had a clear conviction that this was truly a call I had received from God and becoming a bishop was a further way of exercising the priesthood to which I had already been ordained. I knew the tensions that were involved with living a celibate life and yet I knew I could open up to people.

Actually what I have described is not really a very unusual experience. I read an article recently by René Voillaume, the superior of the Little Brothers of Jesus, which talks about this very thing. The article was a kind of letter to all members of the society. He calls the article "The Second Call," and he makes it plain that this sort of thing happens as part of the normal pattern of life for most people who make a commitment at a relatively young age. And when it does happen it is very strengthening and reaffirming of the original commitment. That certainly is the way it has worked for me.

The whole process of naming bishops involves confidentiality and secrecy, so my next step was to reply to the Vatican in some code words that were mentioned in the letter and that would indicate a yes answer. There were no code words for a negative answer. I had to send a telegram back to the Apostolic Delegate. I forget the exact words, but it had something to do with Baptism in the Latin rite.

Once the announcement was made ten days later I began to

wonder to myself, What is it like to be a bishop anyhow? I guess I considered I might be expected to step into some kind of mold and I had a fear of that. So I asked the cardinal if saying yes to this really meant that I had to change the way I had been. Archbishop Hallinan had asked the cardinal the same question years before, and Hallinan was a very common sort of man, very down to earth. He told me what he told Hallinan: "Look, they investigated you before they ever sent you that letter; they want you as you are. So just be yourself. Don't worry about fitting a mold."

I didn't have much of a vision of what I was going to do. I figured I would do a lot of ceremonial functions like Confirmations and ordinations and maybe speak somehow more officially in the name of the church at times, at least in the minds of people. They don't always make distinctions between an auxiliary bishop and one who is *the* bishop of the diocese. I really had a narrow view of the job; I never viewed the appointment as an opening to some kind of national platform. I was vaguely aware that there was such a thing as the National Conference of Catholic Bishops, but it didn't seem to be particularly aggressive, cohesive, or dynamic, and I wasn't upset by that. I just thought a bishop served his own diocese and that's what was most important.

I don't suppose anybody thought very much about my appointment. I was young, yes, but I hardly had any kind of radical reputation. What impressed me most when I attended my first meeting of the NCCB was how ready the men were to accept me, they seemed to want to make me feel a part of the conference right away. But I wasn't that fascinated by the NCCB itself; it was more a case of being impressed by different bishops and what they did in their dioceses. Men like Cardinal Shehan in Baltimore, who seemed very warm, human, and modest and who was doing things with the blacks in his city, like Bishop Flores, Bishop Malone, Bishop Borders, Bishop Gallagher, Bishop O'Donnell, Cardinal Dearden right here.

As I began to try to visualize what my job as a bishop really was it became clear that it was not in being some remote, powerful, authoritarian figure but more like being pastor in a parish, preaching and teaching the gospel and applying it to things that are happening today. As a bishop it seems that the responsibility is simply a bit broader, to speak to bigger audiences about larger issues, although they are essentially the same issues that should be handled in every parish.

Take for example a question like the involvement of the United States in the Vietnam war. I just don't see how you can not have a stance in an issue like that. No stance is actually a stance and I knew I would have to make my position clear regardless of what group I was working in. I had to offer my decision as one man's Christian response to a situation, and then people could decide on its worth. I believe a bishop's standing up for an issue forces Catholics to at least take that issue seriously and, hopefully, to think it through. I never expected hordes of Catholics to follow me—only to think. If they consciously decided the war was a righteous and a moral one, at least they didn't make a decision by default.

Because of my work with parishes throughout the diocese and also in many areas of emphasis in the church, I came into contact with large numbers of people and they continued to hold me accountable when I became a bishop. After a bishop's conference where we skirted the issue of bombing and death in the war, I felt pressure from many of these people. When are the bishops going to speak? they asked me. These were college people, other young guys I'd counseled through a draft situation, a broad range of people in the parishes. In 1971, when the NCCB finally issued a rather strong condemnation of the war, I was quite encouraged and was able to bring some encouragement to many people who were looking to their bishops, who were by vocation moral leaders.

Often I had felt that when bishops got together we were preoccupied with housekeeping chores rather than burning moral issues. First Confession before First Communion or vice versa. Financial difficulties of Catholic schools. I can remember spending an hour in debate over where to file dispensation records under the new regulations for mixed marriages. That is disheartening to me. How does this fit in with the vision of the church as the leaven within American society, bringing about conversion and change?

I would rather see the bishops come together, after having prepared themselves ahead of time, and with resource persons present, like the *periti* at the Council, discuss the real problems and opportunities that confront us today—the advances in medicine or genetics, or changes in sexual attitudes, or the consumer society that keeps so many people continually poor, or our mechanized technological society. What do we do about those problems? Let's bring in people from the Department of Defense and bring in the peace people, take three or four days to hear both sides. So often we beg off from taking a stand because we say we don't know enough about the war to say anything. The conscientious objector has to make a decision, but we're saying *we* can't.

We all know that the situation among American priests is very very serious; numbers are leaving, but even more crucial is that large numbers are unsure of themselves as to what their vocation is. I remember back in 1969 we had a discussion of the priesthood and celibacy and we were going to issue a statement reaffirming that celibacy was the law of the church and everybody just better accept that and obey it. At this point I'm willing to accept that; I'm going to be celibate the rest of my life. But when I talk with priests who are agonizing over this I can't simply say this is the law. They're looking for something more, some rationale that wasn't given to us in the seminary. What's being questioned is the whole theology of the priesthood, and celibacy is just one part of that. There is a clear and articulated theology of the priesthood. The study commissioned by the NCCB provides this. But somehow many lives have not yet really assimilated this theology and been able to integrate their lives on the basis of it. I am very grateful that I have been able to think it through and feel so clearly called by God to this ministry of ordained priesthood. I am happier in the priesthood now than any time in my life. I feel it is really a challenging way to use whatever talents and gifts I have. In the Gospel Jesus makes clear that *he chooses* his disciples. We don't choose this vocation. I just pray in thanks every day that for some reason he has chosen me.

I personally could see the possibility of ordaining married men to serve, for instance, in the Godforsaken areas of the country where there isn't another priest for two hundred miles. But that's quite different from optional celibacy. Celibacy, for me, has to be for life or it isn't celibacy. It is a charism, a sign that certain people choose to make and create a life style revolving around it. And so, to prepare people to live a celibate life, we can't merely say that this is a precondition to being ordained and you have to accept it. I think we have to acquaint people with their human psychology and emotional needs and how friendships are built. Our preparation was more how not to get married. Rather we have to show that friendships can be built in a slow, reciprocal process with another human and that you can gradually open yourself up and let yourself in a sense be vulnerable.

I need friends, male and female. I've always enjoyed being with people, and yet it was hard for me to let people really come into my life, because there was always the worry that something would go too far. But I can't grow as a person unless I love and am loved. Once you have worked through to a clear and convincing rationale for celibacy—something that makes it have very real personal meaning to you, not just a discipline that you agree to observe—then you can make a clear and definite commitment to it. I have been able to do this, and I am grateful for that.

You still are very much aware that there are limits to your relationships and a certain discipline that you have to maintain. You don't allow yourself to get into situations where it's too easy to become emotionally overengaged. Yet you have to come close to people and let them come close to you. That creates tension, and the celibate priest has to live with that tension—just as a person striving to be poor has to live with the tension of having material things, enjoying them, and yet at the same time being disciplined about them so that he maintains real freedom in regard to these things. Being in a kind of tension between opposite attractions seems to be part of what virtues are really all about.

If celibacy is a crucial question to priests—and it is to many bishops too, believe it or not—I believe that authority is equally troublesome. If priests have trouble living with people in authority, they should know that the men in authority are questioning how to live with themselves while they're in authority.

Authority needs a lot of probing, discussing, and developing. We have to separate authority from power. Leadership, not power, has to be the virtue. Authority's first job is to unite, it is not to dictate from a seat of power. Authority must listen and be responsive. It must draw people, not force them. It must create the environment where people can grow into full personhood. Basically authority has to be exercised by someone who is authentic and real. If you're going to lead people without just coercing and without using power over them, then you have to be authentic in your own way of living the Gospel life. That will draw people and cause them to follow.

What is the most common complaint of priests? "I have this conservative bishop and he won't let us do a thing." If that happened to me I would find some way to function while finding some way to convey my convictions to the person in authority. Every priest is charged with the obligation to keep the person who has authority over him responsible. But too often we think we are the final answer, the only answer, and the rest of the world is out of step. But really, if I'm cut off for a while, God can still work His way without me. Look at the theologians who were so instrumental at Vatican II after they had been in an eclipse in the 1950s. Congar, De Lubac, Murray; they were under tremendous pressure, so they just went into a sort of seclusion, kept on writing, and waited for the time to be right. And yet to meet these men you could see they had a very humble attitude toward their work.

I'm not advocating that people roll over and play dead when they feel they are being wronged by people in authority. That's why many dioceses have instituted due process procedures. In Detroit we've handled everything from a janitor being dismissed to the firing of a director of Christian Education to a situation where an assistant felt that the pastor was depriving him of certain rights to preach and teach. In the past the younger man would probably have been transferred. In this case there was a fault on both sides and the only way to do it was to remove both men and bring in somebody else to pull together a very polarized parish. And priests don't have to accept arbitrary reassignments any more.

Looking at authority from a priest's point of view, I don't think his response to his bishop needs to be something so all-pervading in his life that it has to overshadow everything else he does. There is such a thing as responsible obedience—meanwhile the man can function and live out and preach the word. We have to go back to the fact that Roman law is not as authoritarian as it would imply.

The priest has the responsibility to let the person in authority know what the situation is, so that decrees or new rules are not continually made that do not fit pastoral needs. People in a parish have the same responsibility to their pastor-leader, so that parish decrees or directives don't become unreal and unworkable. Through dialogue, through consensus, authority works to unite people.

I think that priests who are rebuffed in their first effort often give up. I think a more mature way is to admit it didn't work that way and to come back at it another way, at another time. Bishops are generally not ogres or completely insensitive or incapable people. So you keep coming back and you do it with patience and calmness and love—and determination. I backed the Berrigans for what they were doing because I saw them going about their protest in a peaceful way and not ending up bitter about it. That got a lot of negative response, because these men are viewed as criminals by some Catholics. I can't buy that, and I have to make a sign that I stand behind them.

Through all this strife that we are in the midst of today, I believe in the axiom of *ecclesia semper reformanda,* the church always in need of reform. That applies to priests and the rest of the church alike, some dying and some coming to life. But it appears that we have waited until problems have hit us over the head before we acted.

Take Catholic education. The system began in 1884 with the ideal of having every Catholic child in a Catholic school as a protection of their faith, because the public schools were teaching Protestant religion. We're approaching 1984, and are the needs the same? We never succeeded in getting all the kids into Catholic schools and now the numbers are dropping. Should we patch up the system or go with something entirely different? We hear about the financial situation within dioceses, but is that all the schools represent? What about investigating sociological, theological, and historical factors?

The bishops authorized this huge $500,000 study of the American priesthood which has told us a vast amount about priests in every possible light. But we haven't done a thing with it. It's published for the most part, but we haven't acted on the information there. We don't want to face out our problems and work through them. I don't know if it's a lack of confidence or faith on the part of us bishops, as though if we looked at a problem it would overwhelm us. Don't we have enough confidence that even though Jesus may be asleep in the boat, he's there and he can lead us through? We're men of little faith who, when you get right down to it, rather than deal with problems, run for cover. And I suppose at some point Jesus is going to wake up and rebuke us. I hope he does.

Father Joseph O'Rourke

Joe O'Rourke's father died two days before he was born. His mother never remarried and he was raised as the only child of a single parent. Typical underpinnings for a vocation, some might say. A strong mother pushing a dependent son into the priesthood where he could be married for life to an institution, thus precluding the need to be wed to another mere woman.

But this small family was different. Joe's mother was a professional woman, a guidance counselor, then the director of pupil personnel in their home town of Hudson, New York. She was as caught up with her work as she was in raising her son, so Joe didn't have an umbrella of overprotectiveness. Within his small town Joe O'Rourke was known as a man for all seasons: a good athlete, model altar boy and chorister, president of his class for six years running, and somewhat of a Romeo who got his share of what girls were allowing in those days.

But even those sins against the sixth commandment, which sent other young boys into confessionals with sweating palms, did not arouse in Joe O'Rourke any enormous sense of guilt. He could say his act of contrition and then spend hours getting the right clothes together and being the star of the dance that night. He feels to this day that it was no mean accomplishment to have three women (his mother was not one) weep when he decided to go into the seminary.

He wanted a "people profession" and seriously considered law, but something about the Society of Jesus appealed to him. As he would recall years later, in the words of Muhammad Ali, "They were not the smartest, just the greatest." Joe visualized himself becoming something of a religious Ernie Pyle with subcareers as a radio announcer and pilot. He knew it couldn't all work out, because he also wanted to marry Margaret O'Brien.

America was settling into the lethargic 1950s when Joe entered the seminary. At that time the Jesuits were billed as the fence busters, the group that was bent on finding the cutting edge and staying there. They were intellectually stimulating but Joe soon found himself uncomfortable with their life style. They could question everything outside their order, but the society itself was off limits. No introspection needed, the sign seemed to say.

He found others within his class who also saw the stupidity of rules that kept them away from the real world. So these young Jesuits began to break the rules or, worse, ignore them.

Joe O'Rourke developed a Robin Hood view of religion, an outlook that was guided not so much by codes as by genuine needs. Mavericks never are well accepted in religious orders, especially before they are even ordained, so Joe on three occasions was told outright to leave. Before ordination he committed a Berriganesque act of civil disobedience—destroying Dow Chemical files, as one of the "D.C. Nine" during the rash of such actions.

He faced squarely whether or not he should be ordained at all. Younger movement people said it would be a copout, akin to joining the Army. But he decided he would press for ordination, so that he could help reform the church from within.

Now thirty-four years old, Joe O'Rourke is a handsome man with dark Irish features and the makings of a beer- and scotch-

nurtured ruddy complexion. He smokes a lot, he is visibly nervous. Although he has many misgivings about the priesthood and the validity of his staying, he feels he must.

I was nineteen and going through the conventional problem of losing my faith—matter of fact I still think I'm losing it about once a month—looking at the stiff morality that I was brought up in and really investigating my notion of God, when I stumbled into the priesthood. I had been looking at law, at business, but already I was having troubles with the institutions that they defended and fostered. Looking at the church as the institution it was, I didn't come out much better. I was looking around for an institution or organization that had the capacity for reforming society (and that essentially has to include the ability of reforming itself), and while the church and most priests were not personally attractive to me, there was something appealing about the basic ethic of the Jesuits. There was this idea called the *majus* or *ad majorem Dei gloriam. Majus* means more and *majorem* means greater. Their ethic was not to be the best or highest but to be better, that is, to constantly reform themselves as they moved into new areas.

We were in the apathetic 1950s, no war to fight, few causes, and everybody was looking for something to dedicate their lives to. The guys I went through the seminary with still muse about it today. We entered in 1958 and we call it the end of triumphalism, because up to that year, from the end of the war, vocations had been rising. After, there was a steady decline. I had been to college for a couple of years and it was tough to go behind the seminary wall. I was involved in campus politics and I also was very close to a woman. Maybe I tended to intellectualize too much and be too tense about my life options, so I went away for a weekend retreat to really think it out.

It was a terrible retreat, but I spent a lot of time by myself. I can remember sitting out by a football field for practically a whole day with a piece of paper and a pencil, writing down the life options and listing the pros and cons. I was mostly afraid to take a risk on religious life. I still think the life is a pretty scary operation. On the plus side I had written down what I had to offer to people through religious life and I came up saying that the biggest difficulty with priests and nuns was that they weren't human enough, didn't smile enough, just didn't get down and dig in with people, and I could do that. When I had to write it down, it came clear that there was a tremendous need in the world for a happy roving band of warriors that would take the Gospel seriously.

On the minus side I saw the institution I would have to work within. It did not take human experience seriously, almost in principle. It seemed hell-bent on proving it had a ball of its own that could be thrown around inside a limited arena. It could play out some special drama apart from the human community. It wanted to justify itself rather than produce a human community, a community of common faith; all "bad cess," as my Irish grandmother used to say.

I was lucky right off the bat in my novitiate in that we had a superior who was kind of a breakthrough liberal, Andy Brady. For example, we didn't have to call each other "Brother" or "Carissime" or speak Latin all the time. But he was a tough guy, nonetheless, like a Thomas More. He straddled two ages, and we can criticize him from either side with the principles of the old or the perspectives of the new. He really was trying to break down hidebound institutionalism, yet it didn't seem as though he was doing it fast enough or with a true alternative vision.

We still held on to some of our medieval practices. Twice a week for two hours in the morning we wore this braided piece of wire with little claws on it around our thighs. Sitting, standing, kneeling, whatever you were doing, this thing was supposed to be on and with every movement there would be pain. Then once in a while we had a particular chapter where each guy would go in front of the master of novices, kiss the floor, and with his arms outstretched would kneel there for ten minutes while every other seminarian would tell about his problems with brother. "Brother tends to be sarcastic, uncharitable," that kind of thing. At other times we heated up things with a little self-flagellation.

It's tough stuff for a nineteen-year-old American to face up to, I suppose, but it was like sports: If he can do it, so can I. You see some little guy walking around in a habit, you know, some simpering wimp, and you say, If he made it, for Christ's sake I can do it too. It sounds weird but it works. Then you get into a deeper thing that that spirituality is based on: pride, self-righteousness, a super masculinity. Add the whole thing of emulation: If brother can do twenty strokes of the whip, I'll do fifty.

But really, if you could get by the penance things and didn't have too much trouble with studies, it was an exciting exhilarating life. Two and a half hours of prayer and study before a breakfast of cornbread and stew and coffee; physical labor, playing basketball that would make Tom Heinsohn look like a Lennon sister. For a young jock in the 1950s it wasn't a bad life.

Already in the novitiate my class was earning a reputation for being, as the master of novices called us, "butter and egg men," you know, salesmen, pushers, doers. Before us, an occasional guy taught catechism in a church, and that was the only apostolic experience off the grounds. We wanted to start local programs, so we got on the phone and expanded our lives to the neighboring towns. The master of novices kept on reminding us that we were novices and had to start taking our spiritual life seriously, get in touch with our roots before we flowered in the world. But basically, it was a case where we could not only not do those things we felt like doing but also those things we felt we *should* be doing.

By the time we hit Shrub Oak up near Peekskill, New York, for our years of philosophy there was already tremendous momentum to expand apostolically and not study philosophy twenty-four hours a day. One wag back then described the closed-in course as a thirteen-year windup for a wild pitch. This was in 1961 and there were already a lot of demons in the air that change was due in the church. Father Henneberry, our superior at Shrub Oak, was a fine old Jesuit who had been in the musical chairs of superiors for a long time and was a commanding man who chopped trees down for exercise and penance. He had gotten perfect marks in every test he ever took as a Jesuit—no mean task—yet he was a man who stressed humility and gentleness. Institutionally, Henneberry was an immovable conservative who bended not at all with the winds of change.

We started to agitate almost from the time we got there. From the ridiculous to the sublime. We wanted to watch the New York Giants on Sunday, and that was a big hassle because it had never been allowed under Henneberry. And we wanted to save Harlem. We began to lean on the system, manipulate it, move it. We looked up the canons and firmed up the legal arguments; we got faculty members lined up who were willing to push the superior. We got to know what we had suspected—that there were not really good reasons to keep us from watching football or working outside the seminary. It was rather a thing of holding the line because, as Cardinal Ottaviani and the reactionaries in the Vatican knew, if you change a little, it all seems to go. In a sense that's true. "It" does go, and you can be afraid of that or you can live in the community conflict, find your principles, your structures in real experience, in people's gut faith, in their power to form a future.

I held the top house job, which was like president of the student body—really it was more a combination union steward and prison trusty—and I'd have to go in every morning at nine-thirty and ask permission for various things for the student body. Totally useless. Ask for this, no; ask for that, no. Anyway, we finally got smart and started to use leverage on him by proposing things that looked pretty simple and irrefutable on the surface but which had larger ramifications. Besides, when things were turned down we began to go ahead and do them anyway.

Three of us started what we called the social apostolate observation program under the guise of getting some knowledge of things that were going on. He couldn't turn us down when we asked to go to parishes and find out why catechism programs were breaking down. Then the butter and egg men moved on and we had cars going to East Harlem Protestant Parish, to New York City's Street Club Project with the gangs. Then we'd come back and have a seminar about it and legitimatize the whole thing. It sounds incredible today that we had to squeeze stuff like that by, but we did. We worked with blacks, drug addicts, and we realized again how incredibly naïve, irrelevant, and narrow was our commitment to our seminary style. It wasn't that we were just on the sidelines watching Kitty Genovese get raped—we weren't just irrelevant—we were doing something worse because we legitimatized a whole structure that stood for something that was separatist, anti-life, anti-future, anti-women, and even anti-Catholic. It was committed to its own self-preservation, its own special salvations, and not committed to helping man.

We looked back and found that St. Ignatius's troop of men weren't committed to seminary life at all or even to education necessarily. They were roving bands of guys who would do almost anything—live with the poor, run around with street women, talk to kings. St. Francis Xavier—talk about a wild rover! Of course he got us tied into the ruling class and colonialism by traveling with the Portuguese imperialists. But the drive was good. Christianity is learning a lot, like it or not, from his "open door" policy. The original Jesuits were really heavy hitters, loners a lot of them, but always trying to find out where the action was; and where it wasn't, they made it. I go on at length about this because Tom Henneberry was a very historically conditioned but aware man who, if he really had seen that the Society and the church were in conflict with the Gospel, would have acted differently.

We seminarians began to see more and more clearly what the conflict was, and if the church didn't know it we were going to put it in crisis. The exodus of men was escalating and we still lived by all these rules that required us to be in for some stupid litany at a certain time and say, "Pray for us," which made us leave some kid we were tutoring up in The Bronx. But for a group of men in our early twenties, we sometimes expressed ourselves in very immature ways. Some men even trained at being Christian crooks, sneaking around the rules, getting up late at night to break into the refrigerator to get a steak. But no one was really threatened by rules any more, and we were going to break as many as necessary to live and act in a community that made sense. Civil disobedience for many was born right there in Shrub Oak.

At Shrub Oak I learned that the Jesuit system was not sacred, that the Jesuits' commitment to intellectual competence was often just a joke because they were so ignorant about how to run an organization dedicated to social change or even how to meet people's needs. Our Ph.D.'s often meant only "phenomenal disinterest." We fought so many hassles that weren't worth fighting.

I didn't take advantage of certain liberties, because of the absurd context. I didn't drink for seven years in the society, because beer drinking was confined to a forty-five-minute period once a week, when guys would try to pound down five beers between the "fun gun" going off and the whistle blowing us into litanies. With the eruptions in the church and society going on outside and this senseless life still perpetuated inside, it really drove us together. There was a big heavy interpersonal thing going on, men feeling themselves out in terms of deeper human emotions, getting in touch with each other now that the system had lost its power. It's really incredible that all good religious don't turn homosexual as they explore the real meaning of interpersonal community with each other. It might even be a good thing.

The options were few if you wanted to remain in the priesthood. You followed the rules, let the questions eat you up, and then let them pay for shrinks for the rest of your life—or you put blinders on. Well, my option was, I suppose, to be a sort of religious Robin Hood. I just found out I had to lead a human life and enjoy it in order to have a religious life; actually they were most often the same thing. One funny story, which doesn't show the severity of this need to steal from the rich for the poor but points out the seminary struggle:

Pat Dexter and I got into a truck we called the Eichmann van—because of the way the exhaust pipe fed right into the back where we carried passengers. There was this big blizzard and we went for a ride. There was a woman over in Tarrytown we were taking a life-saving course from, and there was a Maryknoll buddy of ours close by. So we went over, had a few drinks with the woman, went to a free Maryknoll movie, and then came back to the salt mine, feeling all the better for our little escapade.

We had electric garage doors, so I hopped out in the dark and pressed the button as Dex was driving this van slowly forward with the lights off. He went in too quickly and hit the door with the top of the truck and tore the hell out of it.

For this they made us feel we were letting down 1900 years of tradition. We had to make a three-day retreat in silence, during which we were supposed to contemplate our vocations, because surely anyone who would do such a thing was in doubt. We had to say a *culpa,* a public manifestation of our sins. It goes something like this: "Reverend fathers and dearly beloved brothers in Christ, I say to you my *culpa,* for all my faults and negligences against our Holy Rule, especially for the violation of leaving the grounds without permission, for visiting an extern [anybody who wasn't a Jesuit] without permission, for going fifty miles without permission, and for breaking the garage door without permission." Robin Hood couldn't take all that too seriously, but we could go along with some of the things that made superiors happy.

More to the point, about this time civil-rights action was happening. People outside the seminary were breaking other laws. I was reading Saul Alinsky and I remember seeing *Exodus* and getting really aware of the anti-Semitic reaction and the anti-Israel bias of the Irish Catholics from New York City. They were notorious for calling Jews "kikes" and all that. Reacting strongly to conservative reactions, I began to identify with the more revolutionary spirits. In 1964 I went to teach at Canisius College, one of our middle-class institutions where we make Republican lawyers, and there I really launched into community action work, which would lead up to the first of three times that the Jesuits tried to launch me out of the Society.

I developed a whole bunch of community action programs that eventually had 10 per cent of the campus working in something. All these were the typical Band-Aid programs of the mid-1960s, but they were as good as any and we didn't have any office or funding. People were tutoring, fixing up stuff in the ghetto, taking a census to find out needs, doing road shows for children's homes, getting kids into camps. Really welfare colonialism, but it was a great scene. A buddy of mine, Dick Tyksinski, got involved and he'd run the folk masses and we'd do the social stuff together. We called ourselves Baptism and Robbini, in memory of the old missionary motif. We'd want to get kids into tutoring or to march, so we'd have a party at somebody's house and drink a lot of beer until two in the morning, get into issues, and just give people a hard time until they'd agree to work or to get up the next morning and demonstrate against the racist building trade unions or whatever it was.

Naturally there were women around, a lot of great women; three or four went into the Peace Corps and Vista and then the resistance. It was a great socio-religious scene. I still loved teaching, getting into the heads of these kids, talking about Sartre or Frantz Fanon and giving them some sense of self-worth and freedom so that, no matter what Sister Perpetual Menopause told them back when, they knew they did count and had to make their life decisions seriously.

You are not supposed to have a good time at being a religious, they say; that is a rule we all were supposed to know. I was enjoying being a religious, so they started at me. I was coming in late, missing meals, taking the car out all day. The president of the college finally called me in and told me that I ought to stop what I was doing. What am I doing? You know what you're doing. Yeah, I know what I'm doing but what is it you don't like—women around or me staying up so late, or do you want me home for dinner? No, you know what you're doing. We went around and around like that; I never had a concrete accusation of any sort, just veiled statements like "Having troubles with your vocation, right?"

Well, right then I wasn't. Matter of fact I was kind of enjoying the thought of being a priest.

The next year the Society had to fish or cut bait as to whether or not I was going on to ordination. A lot of the community members wrote very negative reports about my "poverty, chastity, and obedience." And the decision on high was that I shouldn't move on to be ordained.

When my peers heard about it there was a whole flurry of letter writing, and of course I kept on asking what the charges were. The provincial never made any, he just said I should leave the Society. I said no, and he said, "You've got a fourth year of teaching to reconsider your vocation." And in a high school, as if that were a demotion. The "fourth year" is supposed to be a kiss of death for the upwardly mobile Jesuit. They were trying to housebreak me, to rub my nose in it. I sure as hell wouldn't surrender to that kind of punishment. There was a religious view at stake. The new patch in trouble with the old seams.

I really didn't work overly hard at the high school; I'd announced I was there under duress and that I didn't intend to be overly cooperative. Loved the kids I was teaching, but otherwise I spent time by myself or working for the Coalition for a Democratic Alternative or speaking for civil rights and against the Vietnam war. And I was reading more and more. Alinsky was really getting to me about power and powerlessness, and I began to see my life very much in those terms. My struggle, the struggle of my classmates, was really to get the institution back on some kind of community basis.

But then comes the inevitable question once the issue is cut for you: Is this church institution worth the effort, and why in the hell do I have to be a priest to work on our real mission? Basically, of course, I dig the Good Book and the Man, and there are a lot of good people around the institution, and it could be working for good if the right people, all the people, could have some clout. Deep down, *hubris* was at work too. I was not going to lose a bad argument. I didn't want the Roman Catholic Church or the Society of Jesus as it existed to win an argument because I wasn't there.

Oddly enough, that year I was elected by that high school community, mostly priests, to represent them in a provincial reevaluation of all our institutions. Failing manpower and overextension were the problems, but few would drop their vested interests and geographical loyalties to make the necessary big creative changes. They ended up by saying, We've got to change, but we won't. We can't go on the way we're going, but we will.

My whole view of the institution evolved to a point where it clearly became an enemy, and I couldn't wither and run away from the enemy when I felt I should be coming out on the winning side. But it wasn't a very nice life, still a lot of pain from it in my life.

Take the institution of Canisius College and the other institutions that it serves, wittingly or unwittingly. I taught about social ethics in philosophy and had these bright-eyed guys in front of me on Monday in their green suits and little brass buttons. I talked about the war, a perfectly open multiviewed presentation, and with the facts laid out those kids had little doubt that the war was wrong.

Hey, Mr. O'Rourke, that's really interesting about the war. Never looked at it that way; makes a lot of sense. Really got to talk to you about that, but I can't right now. I've got to go off to ROTC drill.

Working on the Coalition for a Democratic Alternative, we decided we had to get somebody to run for the Democratic National Convention in 1968, so I asked this fellow Al Bartlett, a very well known priest in Rochester who was rector of the school. He was willing and agreed to run. The trustees called him and told him, You will be over for cocktails Saturday afternoon. In he walks and all these big businessmen, all regular Democrats, tell him, We're going to take our money out of the school, going to resign publicly, and we are never going to give another penny if you persist in running. So he had to drop out for the school's sake. The contradictions!

By the time I hit Woodstock, Maryland, for my years of theology, seminary was a less important thing to me, and action, doing something, was primary. The institutionalized violence was all-pervasive to my mind. I picked up old friendships with guys that felt the same way. Phil Berrigan was in Baltimore and Dan Berrigan, the Jesuit, had founded Clergy and Laity Concerned About Vietnam and had visited Hanoi. Spellman had gone bananas and had him shipped off to South America, where he got even more into the struggle of the poor. Catonsville happened just before I came to Woodstock, and all of a sudden I found myself looking for something similarly strong that would confront the contradictions in my life and in our society. I had supported civil-disobedience actions, explaining why they were justified. And I was beginning to believe my own rhetoric.

In March of 1969 I went down to Washington with two women and six other men, all of whom but one had a priest or nun history.

One other guy was a Jesuit, Mike Dougherty, who had always been a conservative, temperamentally at least, but a strongly committed religious. He was a guy who woke up one morning and said, No, the war's wrong, and if it's wrong I've got to change it. On a Saturday afternoon we walked into Dow Chemical, the napalm maker, at Fifteenth and L streets—this was their national liaison office with the Pentagon and State Department—and took all their files and threw them out the window in a kind of ticker-tape celebration of a sort, exposing their complicity in murder and exploitation to the public. The D.C. Nine was born.

We were tossed into jail for eight days and a lot of my peers came to visit, but only one of the Jesuit superiors even inquired after our health. The three felony charges were toughest on our families, who didn't understand. My mom was very disappointed at my risking a career and breaking convention. She had never pulled mother tricks, pouting and all that, on me. She was always straight and honest about what she thought I should and shouldn't do. She just called me up at eight o'clock the morning after I was busted and started right off with rational arguments of why this was a stupid thing, that there were better ways to do it—I could have written letters to Dow and so on—and at the end she said, "Besides that, you're fasting. EAT!"

There were rumblings around that I was going to be tossed out for sure this time, and those rumblings started a little revolution in the ranks that I didn't even know about. The province superior confronted me with performing a disobedient act as a Jesuit, and my peers called a public meeting where the superior was asked in to answer the community's arguments. A meeting like that is usually an exercise in futility. The superiors have their minds made up when they walk in, and the inferiors take their licks.

I explained that I hadn't been disobedient, that according to the law of the Society I had informed and consulted my local superior, John Conlin. He and Felix Cardegna, the Woodstock rector, were taking a lot of heat from above. Cardegna, a terrific guy who since has left, was one of the few superiors I've had who knew anything about Gospel obedience. They sat there while the provincial superior, Bob Mitchell, read all the statements on protest we had developed throughout the 1960s, mostly due to Dan Berrigan in some way. These outlined procedures, the whys and wherefores of protest, and he thought they'd show us wrong. After they were read, even the most conservative guys in the community got up and justified us in terms of the statements and religious obedience, although many didn't buy the action.

Mitchell was convinced, but there was a problem with Tom Birmingham, his subordinate, who was a hawk and who already had suggested we leave. Birmingham was then in Rome and the whole business was a problem there. He wanted us to be brought down hard. So Mitchell was caught. While his subordinate was in Rome presenting the hard line Mitchell was brought around by the community, but he said, "I can't do anything about this now, because, while I'm the ultimate authority here, I don't want to override him." They didn't let him off: "You're Birmingham's boss. You've called Rome before, you can call again."

Up to that point we had a ban of silence on us which was now lifted, and it became clear the Jesuits weren't going to throw us out into the street. We didn't really want to go back to school at Woodstock; we wanted to get out on the road and organize. I made some sounds about my studies, took an exam or two, but for the most part I avoided the whole scene and spent a lot of the next six months with Phil Berrigan. We just talked to people about what we had done and why, and more things like it began to happen. A lot more. I rapped throughout the Southwest that summer, going into places where not many peace creeps had been before. I got to Texas—Dallas—and spoke to a crowd that included General Walker, the guy who brought in the troops for Orville Faubus and who passed out the John Birch literature to our Army troops in

France. He asked the classic question: If you guys can do it to Dow, why can't I go into a peace office and disrupt the files? I explained to him the principles of civil disobedience and nonviolence and said, "Fulfill those and you can." He really dug the answer, although hard put to meet any of the conditions, and gave us a dollar donation.

I went to Alinsky's Industrial Areas Foundation in Chicago the next summer and helped organize Polish Catholics on the South Side who were fighting corporations and other institutions down on their lives. Then the Harrisburg Eight fiasco broke, and I worked to raise bail and set up a defense committee. Other nonviolent actions were occurring, and we spent time just getting people out of jail.

Every once in a while I'd show up at Woodstock and say, Hey, I'm interested; I'm being a religious; I think I could be a priest. Three or four good friends on the faculty were for it, so they talked with the provincial and he talked with me and said maybe we'll ordain you if you do a couple things, like a reading program to make up for your lost study time. I said, Well, maybe I'd do that, but to tell the truth I didn't do much academically. Instead I read and discussed a lot about the religious and sacramental dimensions of resistance. Some friendly priests were part of an examining board, and we more or less rapped for a few hours and they passed me as ready for the diaconate in December of 1970 with ordination to follow in June.

Just two days before ordination came the third time they tried to steer me out of the priesthood. My superior claimed he had overheard a conversation about celibacy I had the night before with a bunch of men close to ordination. Someone told me later that one of the men had actually reported me, and the conversation.

Everything he quoted back to me was substantially what I believe. Being for optional celibacy notionally is not enough, for even the discussion of celibacy and its alternatives couldn't go on until each priest said to himself and said in public, Yes, I'm sexual; I'm doing it; I'm relating sexually, and these are the real religious problems I'm experiencing. The conversation always dances around that and the arguments go off into space, but in the back of everybody's mind is the question: Is he having a sexual relationship or not, or if this law was repealed would he, could he, start? There is a kind of fear and unfaced risk, a celibacy, even in the discussion.

I told him I had no problems about religious men having sexual relations before ordination and I wouldn't have them after. The trouble with institutionalized celibacy is that it rejects a complete faith, excludes certain kinds of people and experiences. To my way of thinking, a full physical experience of another person is a human and religious demand at times. There are certain times when you've got to be able to express your love fully, whatever way, that's all. Otherwise, your love and commitment to a loving society is in question. We teach the communitarian nature of the Gospel, yet in celibacy we deny common humanity and institutionalize not only an a-religious but an anti-religious routine. It's when you are confronted by an allegedly intelligent man like a superior giving you all the phony buttressing arguments for a dead issue that you just want to bail out.

That kind of discussion naturally brings an institutionalized superior to say, Mr. O'Rourke, do you honestly believe you have a vocation? That's not a word I really like in this context; institutions don't call. John the Baptist cries out still and Jesus demands the truth that frees. Still. And the community calls for response to its needs, and that's vocation, special charism, oil, grease enough. To routinize loneliness, in any way, seems to be against all that. Loneliness is a fact for many of us, but the only good reason for it ever is our commitment to reunion.

That seemed to satisfy him so he didn't stop the ordination. But there were other people doubtful, from a much more humane perspective. I was one of the doubters, but I'll explain that a bit later on. There were fifteen of us, including Tony Meyer and myself, ready for ordination, which was to take place in the Fordham chapel and was to be done by none other than the military vicar himself, Cardinal Cooke. Tony had been on the West Coast, a beautiful freaky man with long hair who wears jeans and a Roman collar. He was active in the movement and he didn't want any part of Cooke; he wanted Bishop Parilla from Puerto Rico, the Independentista. The superiors weren't up for that.

The day of ordination Tony and I passed out sheets with Cooke's picture and the song "Sky Pilot" on them, which is a scathing criticism of military chaplains. We had talked over what we had to do, because at the ceremony we just couldn't go through the thing as if Cooke shared no formal complicity with the killing in Vietnam. At the time when we were supposed to give the cardinal the kiss of peace, Tony went right over to the microphone and said he was not going to do it until Cooke resigned his military vicariate, stopped his investments in military contractors and his whole complicity with the government in this immoral war.

It was a very tight scene there in the chapel. Our families were there; I had had so many hassles with the priesthood just getting there. What I did was one of the hardest things I ever did in my life. Harder than the D.C. Nine action. I was brought up not to break windows; I was brought up to be nice in church. I stood up and said to Cooke, "I find it difficult to kiss peace with war, and I ask you to resign your military vicariate, drop your war-related investments. But I wish you peace. Peace in the end."

Cooke came running over to the microphone when Tony was up there and won it from him by just being very cool, droning on that he was only involved in the spiritual care of the fighting men. In a sense, Cooke won that little confrontation with a little pontifical prevarication. We had succeeded in making the provincial Mitchell angry again, but offended also was John Gallen, who was very helpful in getting me ordained. He was one of the examiners, for example, but was also liturgical coordinator of the ordination. Mitchell was furious; Gallen was personally hurt. Mitchell said if anything more "happened" in the near future, that was it; I was out. Then back in the sacristy when we were unrobing after the ceremony one of the guys said in a loud voice, "Tony and Joe, you chose to make your statement in public. I make mine in private. You wrecked the day our parents have waited twelve years for." You don't want many days like that one.

I had had real problems personally with getting ordained anyhow. A lot of my resistance friends really think the church is part of the "pig," and they're not really wrong. To a lot of young people my getting ordained meant my justifying the church establishment. In the eyes of my superiors, it could have legitimatized the institution as relevant. If O'Rourke still digs it enough to be ordained, there's a reason for the church to stay the same. The only way I could explain it was that in some sense my getting ordained steals back the priesthood for the people. The church has been telling people what Christianity means, what priesthood means, and they don't live up to those things, don't even want to. The issues are going to be cut by the very fact that resisters to the institution are going to make it do our thing. That is to say we will redefine the priesthood on the spot, as we did in the ordination ceremony.

I am recognized as a religious person within some communities of Christians. Within the resistance community I'm recognized as religious, an interpreter and celebrator who remembers the Gospel. That kind of priesthood calls me to do certain things, and I talked about some of these when I said my first Mass. I would be a person to officiate at "sacraments," which are public announcements celebrating moments teeming with future, with possibility, pregnant with the Gospel thrust. Births, deaths, a new love, an act of civil disobedience. Unless I had gone through a lot of things in the resistance—*the* Gospel life in our time—over a period of years that helped me reinterpret my traditional block and tackle, I couldn't have said that, been comfortable with "being a priest." Perhaps I couldn't have fought to be ordained.

From that day, the priesthood has been a very tricky thing for me to deal with because, although I shouldn't admit this, I'm kind of a closet priest, whipping it out when it fits the community struggle, and not always when it's "useful" or expected. To me the expression of my Christianity right now is resistance, nonviolent, comprehensive community resistance, and I have to continually square that up with the book and talk about it. Being the conventional image of the priest doesn't do this and can reinforce anti-Gospel attitudes.

I know that I can be continually held off at arm's length by the Jesuits because they know they can't "trust" me or expect me to stay within certain conventional limits. Like Dan. After Dan Berrigan got out of prison he bounced from the Jesuit provincial house in the Bronx to a couple other places before the Protestants up at Union Theological Seminary took him in. Berrigan is being what a Jesuit means. The felonious monk. Jesus was a burglar too, went around stealing corn on the Holy Day. He disrupted the temples of stone and sterility, and we have a positive command from the Gospel to be disruptive when a moral value is at stake. Are there other ways to attack institutionalized problems of our times? Sure. Are these last resort–type actions? Sure. We tried other ways and they don't work at the moment.

Priests aren't generally willing to take effective means to change things, or even themselves. We won't challenge the securities of the present system, which is corrupt in principle and eating away at all of us. We have to announce that we have no personal stake in this society as it is any more. Not pay taxes. Organize challenges to our corporate mammons, take the jail resulting from simple action-statements of truth. That's the only way the lions in Washington recognize what's going on. The Harrisburg trial made them look like fools to the people. Catonsville did too. I hope the D.C. Nine will as well—they don't seem to be able to get me into jail. The real job, it seems to me ever since Gospel days, is to feed the lions to the Christians.

So, as a person does battle against the violent institutions, he finds he lives a life of constant contradictions, and harder, a life with no secure base, where meaning is a make-it-up-fast enterprise. When you don't put your trust in money or your money in trust, what do you do? Put your trust in trust I guess. I can still live a comfortable, middle-class life while the Gospel tells me to give all I have and live in poverty. I get $150 a month and I can live well enough, but it may not last. Also, I live a contradiction about women, in that there are women all over in my life. The distinction between hangers-on, Christian freewomen, community people, and lovers isn't always clear. Women are a part of our Jesus community. They were part of his; they'll be part of ours. And that means openness to sex as a way of relating and, of course, the risk and responsibility such a relationship should imply. Marriage isn't presently part of my agenda. I've got problems with that institution too, but for sure I feel celibacy is an institutional negative.

The chauvinism of the being-liberated priest is unbelievable; we're really more comparable to black revolutionaries coming out of a matriarchal society. As one priest friend of mine put it, "Women's liberation? I'm just beginning to enjoy chauvinism." We easily trample over people, use women. And the collar can be the greatest come-on in the world for getting close. You talk about celibacy and just get sensitive to each other; it's as sure-fire as the line of male experts on women's liberation. That's a part of me I hate to face.

There's a whole kind of resistance that needs to be done to work on people's heads and hearts about priests' relationships with women. Like Dermie McDermott down there on the Lower East Side. Seen with one woman "too much," they remove his faculties and then cut off his pay. He made them fry for it. Went down and applied for welfare the next day, stood in line like a welfare mother, got put off like everybody else, and then went on a talk show to expose the church and the welfare department. He's still living in the rectory down there as a fine witness that he will not be shoved aside because of some exclusive canons and conventions about priests which demote the other half of the human race.

I can't resist everything at once, so I'm presently concentrating on trying to acquaint church institutional investors with their own responsibility and capacity to challenge systemic sin. Religious shareholders are, for example, challenging corporate management on their presence and support of apartheid in South Africa, their Ford plant in Saigon, their production of anti-personnel weapons. Why does Gulf Oil have to support the expenses of the colonial war against the Angolans, for instance? We aren't running in and disrupting corporate offices just now. We merely point out what they're doing, ask for change, go to the stockholders' meetings, then go in like Clergyman Goodbody Sweet Pants and play it cool. That kind of stuff is very threatening to them. They are not dumb, they're mildly responsive, they sense there's a people's movement around the face of the earth; we Christian people are and should be a part of it, and the corporations don't want to lose us.

Some people say the Gospel gets lost in all this. I don't think so. When we go to a Dow stockholders' meeting and show napalmed babies with gangrene, that's got to work on people's heads. The Gospel's clear about indiscriminate means of war. The Holy Innocents are part of our conscience. That kind of inhumanity doesn't take a lot of translating. So the businessmen get upset. We've got to be practical, they say; you can say all that stuff because you have a collar on. I take the collar off and hand it to them. You put it on, see if it makes a difference in the facts, in who's a murderer.

As options go, I think this is a good job, but if I didn't get the Jesuits to somehow sanction it, to pay some support of it, I'd be letting the institution off too easy. So I asked them to support the corporate-responsibility apostolate. That makes it an institutional commitment down my road, down the road of the poor people's movements where they don't find it particularly easy to go. I think there is a fantastic future in institutional religion, as much as I knock it. Few people around believe me when I say that; they think I just want to tear everything down. No, because if the Society of Jesus in the United States was willing as an institution to say it's against the war and effectively live on that, educate people, attack governmental foreign policy, hassle corporations that are accomplices to the war, send missionaries to help in revolutionary movements abroad, we could be changing things.

I stay a priest simply because I am one. Most younger men like myself in the "institutional" priesthood today have no security hangup about leaving it or staying within it. It is no longer a big enormous threatening thing to get out of this whole chaos that is the institutional church. I've had four or five years without all those institutional buttresses and platforms and tentacles. It's not a success trip, of course, and the real difficulty and the real purpose is still to steal the book back for the people. If I have any vocation or vision at this point, that's about what it is. Because Cardinal Cooke owns the book, owns the meaning of religion right now. Nixon supported Catholic schools and he came out against abortion; don't think Cooke and Krol didn't pay their dues for that. Al Bartlett up in Rochester got the squeeze, Nixon gives Cooke the squeeze, Cooke squeezes him back. Power games back and forth, and the book doesn't even get used. The bishops own the book and they own slum dwellings, so the book must be used to reinforce the present authority structure or else they lose their slum dwellings.

Matthew and Mark are pretty much sitting in the enemy camp right now, and we have to get them back, read their book, live it, write the next chapters of Christ's life. The church still stands more for quiet than for peace.

What basically I have to do this year as a priest within this institution called the church is create collision in the ruling class—good Marxist view—to get the establishment institutions hassling one another, to create some relief from power for the poor. But we must raise issues within the church that are a lot more substantial than whether or not to vote the GM stock proxy. We have a big education job to go back and repeat all this work for new constituencies as they emerge. When Dan got out of jail and all those nuns from Staten Island were there, you just knew there were new people ready to listen, ready to help you steal back the book. Land and food co-ops, housing paid for by land sold by the church, nonviolent group work, gut-issue reorganizing. I think an accurate reading of the Gospel would make Jesus a nonviolent revolutionist, and we have to train people in that image. People are ready. Len Dubi got the Chicago Polacks marching down to Campbell Soup to give them hell about the smokestacks that were poisoning their "Campbell's Kids." Then the next day, with Irish and black together hunkering over plans like a Christian crap game, there was a march with Len to the Board of Education to protest crowding in the classrooms. That's a vision of the parish priest if you want one.

Or take a guy like Ken Feit, who just signed his papers to get out of the Jesuits because he wants to spend full time being a fool. His card reads "Ken, a fool." He's a professional clown, kabuki dancer; he goes over to Central Park, puts on the white face and juggles, has a flea circus, and just goes where people need a fool, a mirror to their meaning. He priests with that whole thing, blows people's minds, he makes them smile just because they are alive.

Most people don't understand Kenny, I don't expect to be understood much either. The priest is in a very queer position, and if anybody is a walking contradiction in America today, he is. I am.

part three

Of Mortal Flesh: Women in Their Lives

"The priest is supposed to be the man up there with all the answers, and here is one going through a deeper crisis than most of the people who look to him for stability. But in these pains I come to the point where most people are at, and I can relate to the kind of faith and hope I tell them to have. Until you are broke, until you miss a woman's touch, you shouldn't be talking to a man who just lost his wife or a divorced woman trying to put her life together."

—FATHER ROBERT ROH

"It was the idyllic, fairy-tale week together. Time ceased. No past, no future. Just me and her. God, it was beautiful. Something out of time and space. Well, how do you fall in love gracefully? And a priest with a nun? We were like two teenagers. We just wanted to be with each other every minute. Just to be able to reach out and touch the other person at any moment."

—"FATHER BILL"

"Maybe it was a period of rebuilding, a re-creation, a discovery of what kind of norms I would follow, because you just can't come out of a seminary and find yourself in an affair with a woman—liking it and not feeling guilty—and not wonder what the hell is going on in your life."

—"FATHER JEROME KILLEEN"

Father Robert Roh

When boys Bob Roh's age were still relegated to the humiliating farm chores of feeding chickens or gathering eggs—girls' work—Bob was able to hop up on the tractor and drive it until the Nebraska fields were dark. When it came to football, he made All-State in his junior and senior years. When it came to good looks, he had them. Girls at the David City, Nebraska, High School would melt when this blond god showed his blazing white straight teeth and smiled their way.

By the time of his high school graduation Bob was nearly six feet tall, weighed two hundred pounds, and colleges and universities were offering him both athletic and academic scholarships. He liked that. He liked being acclaimed, being sought after. He had learned how to insure that success, to make sure awards and gold stars came his way. Basically, he pleased people—with his effort, his good looks, his earnestness. Bob Roh was already very good at pleasing those in authority when he made a career choice and entered the seminary in 1957.

He entered for a strange combination of reasons. He did want to serve people in some yet unformulated way. And, coming from a family where his father was constantly plagued by overdrawn checks, bad crops, or sinking beef prices, he wanted security. A football player might break a leg, a businessman might have a bad year, but a priest would never go wanting; and in the mentality of the mid-1950s he was assured a place of respect throughout his lifetime.

He enrolled at Notre Dame but soon transferred to St. Benedict's College in Kansas. At Notre Dame the austere surroundings and curtainless windows hadn't fit the priestly image. At St. Benedict's he set out in his usual methodical way to be the best possible seminarian he could be, and he did so well there he was sent to Catholic University on a fellowship. After a period of adjusting to the more demanding studies at Catholic U. he again picked up his pace and excelled and was eventually selected for study in Rome. In Rome he was named head of his class and was honored by ordination six months early. Bob Roh had recognition, he had success; he had worked hard for them and he had got what he was after.

Although he was in Rome at the time of the Vatican Council and some of his fellow seminarians had already sensed what it forecast, Bob Roh marched to the safe, ancient drummer. After living in a rarefied intellectual world for so many years, he returned to Nebraska to his first assignment, still listening to that drummer. He was ready to serve, to teach, to obey. He knew he must do that to obtain the ultimate goal, the ultimate sign of recognition that he sought. Bob Roh frankly wanted to be a bishop and was prepared to do all the things necessary to achieve that end.

His first assignment and then a job working in the chancery office exposed him to the real church, with its dailiness, its ugliness, its politics. Bob Roh found himself less and less willing to follow rules for their own sake. First to himself, then to fellow priests, then to laymen, he began to complain, to "bitch about the system" that seemed to put its own preservation above the common good. It began to sink in that he, Bob Roh, had been a willing hand-

maiden of that system for years. Because the system had acknowledged him, rewarded him, he had been more than willing to serve it. But he began to realize that the church's pats on his head weren't as comforting as they once were.

A two-week seminar at Notre Dame signaled a turning point. Bob Roh was forced to look inward, to take stock. What he found was that he had little concept of himself as a person, that his priesthood had been built on sand. He also found he could love. He came back to Notre Dame to continue studies and found himself growing more deeply involved with a woman. He wanted to break out of the traces the church had placed on him that in times past he had accepted; he wanted to leave the priesthood.

He knew he couldn't make a sensible decision in that highly charged atmosphere, so he returned to a parish in Lincoln, Nebraska, and at the age of thirty-three gave himself six months to decide whether he could—or should—remain a priest.

Six months passed between the first interviews with Bob Roh as recorded on this page through page 214 and his thoughts as recorded on pages 214 through 217. In the latter segment he tells how he came to his decision.

There was an old nun who used to come out for two weeks of summer school catechism when I was in grade school, and she would dress up one of the boys in little vestments and let him play priest with the wafers and everything. The class would kind of go along with this whole thing. "You shall be a great priest," she told me once as she put the vestments on me. Then one summer another kid was chosen to be the priest and I was really angry. He was stupid and dumb and fat, and just because he was a year older he got to be the priest. Didn't she see I really deserved it? I was a perfect kid, top of my class, and while I never really thought about being a priest, that was the status symbol for that moment and I wanted it.

As I sit back and look at it, the church as I knew it caught me up in the awards syndrome. I was perfect material because I am a proud person; I want acknowledgment.

I don't think the "awards-seeking me" came out until I was well into the seminary, because in grade school and high school most things came rather easily and the rewards rolled in without too much effort. In high school I ran with the disciplined non-smoking, non-drinking do-gooder crowd. We didn't date that much; sure, there was the usual light necking going on, but nothing really serious. And when I did date I had the top girl in the class, best-looking, best student.

The jock in me was very strong; I liked to think about playing college football; I could even envision myself as an All-American someday. For two years I was named to All-State teams in Nebraska newspapers. But there was something inside that kept at me: What would it profit a man to gain the whole world and suffer the loss of his soul? I could not lose my soul.

My father, who was in his late fifties then, was in bad shape financially after losing two corn crops in a row, and the strain of making ends meet was ever present. One summer we had a beautiful crop ready for harvest and a "sirocco" came in from the south and turned the corn from green to brown in three days. I must confess I didn't like the thought of scraping through life.

When I was in high school at David City they were putting up a new elaborate rectory. In our home the only rug was a worn one in the living room, and we had a potbelly stove for heat. The priests had wall-to-wall carpeting and central heating, and no matter how many corn crops failed they still were going to eat. And so, after my senior year retreat, I signed up with the Holy Cross Fathers at Notre Dame, Indiana. The football aura was there, but when I arrived the surroundings were drab. Hell, we had curtains at home and they didn't have them in this old dormitory we had to live in. And I found I couldn't play football anyhow. I left, and soon I was studying for the diocesan priesthood at St. Benedict's in Atchison, Kansas.

At St. Benedict's I never asked any questions about the priesthood. I did have a need to serve people, but VISTA and the Peace Corps weren't around yet. I had seen priests comforting families after a death and being in a role that people looked up to. In the confessional a priest could help a guy get through the guilt of masturbation or whatever was on his mind, and I thought that I would like to help people in some similar way. Also I'm sure there was a certain heroism that I was hungry for. Look what Roh was giving up!

Before St. Benedict's I had never really studied, I had never really been rejected, I had, for all practical purposes, never felt real pain. My exposure to literature had been a jock's exposure, and I could answer test questions without ever finishing a book. At St. Benedict's I got called down for using double negatives and got an F on a term paper. This was a traumatic thing for me; someone said I wasn't God. I couldn't go out for sports, so I went all the harder into the academic life. It came slowly, but I did it. I got great grades and ended up close to the top of the honor roll.

The bishop got me a Basselin scholarship—the first for anyone from our diocese—and I went to the Catholic University of America for my three years of philosophy. I was told there were only twelve given out in the whole country, but when I got to CU I found the number was thirty-five. But at home I still told everyone it was twelve.

Now I was competing with people out of good schools from all over the country—guys who picked up *Brothers Karamazov* not just to get three names for a test but to read the damn thing. I just didn't click there at all. At first I didn't feel I was accepted by the faculty. My perception of the way people viewed me was this: a small-town Bohemian farmboy who was living in the midst of sophisticated men. There was a lot of joking about me—the hayseed, the clumsy one—and about my rather open nature, which can come off as naïveté.

Academic prestige was again eluding me; I had the valedictorian hunger and nothing to feed to it. At the start I was working in the bottom 50 per cent of the class. Although the courses and my whole world were very abstract and artificial, I didn't have the sense to rebel. I thought that this was the way it should be, must have to be. If I had to put on different forms, different codes, develop a different way of living, wear masks in order to be a priest—and I really did want to be the best priest I could be—I would trust the situation and do what was required. I wasn't sensitive enough to the fact that something wasn't sitting right in me. I thought any doubts I had were my problem.

The most painful part was that the first two years of the philosophy course were without any exaggeration an abomination. What people paid $2,000 a year for! To get indoctrinated into the framework of thirteenth-century thought that had been painted over by seventeenth- and eighteenth-century thought. And those existentialists—men like Camus and Heidegger—they were obviously the worst. Obedient Roh nodded in agreement as they were being set up like ducks in a shooting gallery. Some of the sharper boys weren't as easily put aside, but I was one of the sheep.

It was all part of an educational system that kept you satisfied in your little box. You never had to go out and ask the "why" questions. I allowed myself to be programmed with a negative regard for anything that wasn't Catholic. It wasn't that I didn't read non-Catholics, I didn't even want to read them. Why fool around with someone who didn't have the truth?

It was just this year that I pulled out the volume of Harvard Classics with Machiavelli, Thomas More, and Martin Luther. What a threesome! For the first time in my life I read Luther's ninety-five theses and read his letter to the German nobility—and holy cat! His extreme humility, his almost sycophantic attitude toward the bishop—"Your most excellent highness"—and how he slowly comes to this anger and then the "whore of Babylon" talk. I can identify with the anger inside him; I can feel the scars of the system inflicted on him as they were on me.

At CU Roh did eventually triumph. I studied like hell and I graduated with honors. Looking back, the cracks in my walls must have started there as my world was slowly enlarged. In the final year I had a layman, Dr. Cooper, who began the awakening process. Don't know how they let him in, but he was constantly saying to us, "Push it, aggravate it, scrape it, make sure it stands up to the test." I was doing my master's thesis under him—"*Natura Communa:* The Nature of Common Essence in the Writings of Avicenna"—and things started to pile up. One side of me said that thesis was very meaningful and the other side of me said it was hogwash. But I had to push on to get the golden apple.

I got sick while home on vacation, and the frustration level was at an all-time high when I called the girl I had nobly left behind five years before when I went to the seminary . . . at least according to public appearance. And there she was, at my side, consoling me. It wasn't that I wanted to ring out the wedding bells or anything, but I knew I was doubtful about continuing my studies for the priesthood. Back I went to the seminary, but soon after I got there I found myself walking toward the train station to buy the ticket home. I was playing a game and I was sick of myself.

A priest from my home diocese who was doing graduate work at CU was taking his laundry out, and he caught up with me. This man had a great influence on me; to me he was a very holy man, something of a guru. I told him I was going home, I didn't know why, but I thought I'd had it. He grabbed me and took me down to O'Donnell's for steak and lobster and we talked until two that morning. He insisted that the will of God was not something I discovered within myself or within the talents I seemed to have. It was very clear to him that what the system did was the will of God. They weren't kicking me out and that was evidence that it was the will of God that I stay. Fat chance I had of being kicked out. This same man is married now and I'm sure he wouldn't buy his words today, but he believed them then and I did too. I can laugh at it all now, but not without some resentment of how brainwashed both of us were.

Three years later I was walking to my ordination to the subdiaconate and I had about ninety steps to walk up to enter the church of Ara Coeli at the north end of the Roman Forum, and I remember the early morning sun streaming down on the steps. I looked back and said, half serious, half jokingly, to myself, Holy cow, somebody kick me out. Please, I only got five more minutes.

When I was selected to study at the Gregorian University in Rome, all the doubts and all the problems with playing a role were stuffed into the back room again. I had earned an honor, the recognition I had worked for, sacrificed for. And, although I would never have said it to anyone, it was in the back of my mind that this could lead to bishop. Half the American bishops had studied in Rome; it certainly didn't decrease your chances.

I arrived in Rome on October 1, 1962, and on the eleventh the Council began. While some of the more astute guys were plumbing what the Council was about, old Roh was reading the rule book to see what he had to follow. To get B, I had to do A. So I wore my hat two inches above my eyes; I had a cassock on after ten; I wore a bathrobe to go down to the john; I wore the knickerbockers faithfully under the cassock. I guess that rule was to prevent us from taking the cassock off and running down to the local hot shop without people noticing. We traveled in cameratas, groups of eight, so we could safeguard one another's virtue. If I was obedient I was holy, and the biggest rewards would surely come to the holiest seminarian.

Our classes and our texts were in Latin. I was one of the poorer Latin students at the beginning. The discipline of athletics came through, and I'd put my teeth into a hunk of Latin and just sit until I had it. The really intelligent guys soon found out that the amount learned didn't come close to compensating for the effort, so they started to cut from class and started reading Schillebeecks and Rahner and attending only the classes they felt were worthwhile. The rest of the time they studied on their own, reading in a sidewalk cafe with an espresso or locked up in their rooms.

This isn't to say that we didn't have great teachers at the Greg. But the quality of the class didn't matter. I had been conditioned not to be selective, to just be there, get the pencil out, and sit there every day looking at the teacher, face to face, eyeball to eyeball, taking notes, piling up 180 days of daily attendance. I'd walk into the exams, sit down; we'd smile at each other and the teacher knew that I was a loyal son.

As the Council progressed, the Greg loosened up. Some guys benefited by it and took to independent study, others turned bitter, antagonistic, and spent most of their time bitching about the system. There was talk about the impossibility of reform, the need to scrap everything. This talk generally turned me off. Yet at the time for me the Council meant there would be some external changes—we might move the center fielder in fifty feet. I didn't realize that they might start using three or four extra players or that the foul lines would be expanded or that you might start pitching from second base.

In my second year in Rome I was named head sacristan. With the bishops and cardinals coming over, I got to set out the lilies and light the incense; another prestige symbol to me. In my last year I was named first beadle—the man who took care of registering students, handling grades and examinations, working out scheduling difficulties. But the sweetest plum was that I was selected with five others to be ordained six months before my classmates. I would never have admitted it to them, but that meant a lot to me. The Nebraska farmboy from the backwoods schools made it big.

Some of my friends took me out to celebrate with a great meal at Squacerelli's in Frascati. It was a great celebration; each of us downed a liter of wine. Going home, we decided to go swimming in Lake Albano. We rented a boat, piled into it, and rowed out to the middle and stripped naked. The plan—to swim off the booze. Suddenly a helicopter came over. It flashed into my mind that what we were doing might cost me everything I was celebrating.

The other guys got back in the boat before I could and they started rowing toward shore. "We got you now, Roh," they hollered at me. It was all going—head seminarian, the early ordination. About twenty yards from the shoreline it was shallow enough to stand up and they finally gave me my shorts. Those guys were really beautiful as I look back. They knew me; they knew how uptight I was about the rules. They really took me where I was and helped me learn to live a bit more human life—a life bigger than a code of laws. They are the ones who are going to survive in the church today.

It was hard for me to become friends with the more creative, "rule-breaking," independent people. Many of them must have seen another side to me, because they offered me many opportunities to get close to them in school and on trips, but I kept them at a distance. They constantly reminded me that there was more to life than a smooth-running system. They were an important part of my education in Rome.

Those 250 guys I went to school with were a powerful brotherhood, a great community. The reinforcements were constantly there, and never did I experience the cost and frustration of celibate living as I was to after I left the seminary. "Oh, Lord, let my eyes not see that which is vain and sinful; if I do, forgive me." That kind of prayer was said every time we ventured out in our groups, so we wouldn't be contaminated by the outside world and, implicitly, by a shapely leg or beautiful Italian bust. That creates an attitude; whoever programmed the damn thing really did a good job. I really believed that outside the walls were sinners to be saved, people who were screwing every night and getting drunk. O lucky world, to have me coming to save you!

Rome was good to me, fulfilling, really beyond anything I could have imagined for myself. The city taught me to think and taste history. The Italian life taught me that the American way to life and fulfillment was one of many. I never have regretted the total experience and am still deeply grateful to Bishop Casey for sending me.

I said my first Mass in vestments Pius XII had used, with his chalice and paten. Now I smile at it; then I was in awe. But honestly I never was that enthralled by the ceremonies; the homily and the looser liturgies that were just beginning to be possible held great appeal. I might have been a suckling pig on the teat of church authority, but I felt ready to meet people at their level—Latin for the Polish grandfolks and wide open liturgies for kids—when I got back to the States to my first assignment.

I went to Beatrice, Nebraska, and there was a great variety of work. The state home for 2500 retarded kids was there, two hospitals, a tiny high school, a good parish. I could do everything; I was a superstar. I was an instant authority on everything from hospitals to marital counseling. The parish was really a team effort with three or four nuns that worked very closely with us. The pastor was a good man, but caught between the old style and the emerging new. Among his directives was a strict rule that I was not to visit in homes. I held to that pretty well until one nice couple had moved in. I said to hell with him and I was going to visit them. But I felt so guilty the next morning I had to go in and confess to daddy that I had violated one of his rules.

He played the role I put him in—angry parent. I was likable, young, energetic, and I slowly learned that the pastor was to be responsible for keeping the assistant in line. It was very important to him for the parish to see us as a team. Personal contacts were seen as a danger to his position as pastor. The assistant might be more popular and turn the parish against the pastor. I pretty much lived by the rules of the house.

In the spring of 1968 the new bishop asked me to take a chancery job. The bishop probably saw this overachieving young athletic-type guy whom he could possibly mold into his likeness. Chancery jobs often proved to be steppingstones and I knew that, so I was eager to make my mark there. The eleven months and two weeks in this job convinced me that God was not always alive and well in the church. I was vocation director, and getting vocations in 1969 was like selling Edsels. I got two guys to come in, while eight priests left, two of whom were the priests who had offices on either side of me. I was the diocesan director for the National Association for Childhood and was asked to perpetuate the business of ransoming pagan babies. Kids would collect money in their classrooms, and for every ten dollars they got to name a baby that a missionary baptized. I objected to this kind of foolishness and wrote the national headquarters recommending a revision of the whole thing. "Father, this technique has worked for years to make us thousands of dollars, and while theologically you may be correct, it will cost us a lot of money" was the answer to me. My bishop didn't seem to understand my objection.

We were supposed to take our meals with the bishop, and I began to see people who would criticize and object to his programs suddenly modify their positions when he walked into the room. You were yourself and expressed yourself at personal expense. When you moved from behind your mask and expressed a personal opinion that ran contrary to the bishop's view of the world, you were suspected of disloyalty.

It came to the point that our every encounter was a hassle.

When *Humanae Vitae* came out I proposed that the bishop push it to the same degree he pushed Pope Paul's encyclical *On the Development of People,* which talks about overabundance and redistribution of wealth. His response was no response. Then he came into my office one day and saw a copy of the *National Catholic Reporter,* which he had forbidden priests in the diocese to receive. "What is this? I don't want it in the chancery," he said.

In a negative way that year in the chancery was a great experience in that it put me so close to the fire that it made me sit back and think. Up to that time I had no way to discover what I was really angry about. I bitched, but it was a childish bitch of one who has to get it out of his system but who will never change anything. I changed in my year there; the chancery did not change. I didn't want a ministry devoid of a bishop, but I began to sense there might be a juridical minimum I needed to be in contact with him. I knew I had to be in touch with the chancery on essentials, but it was creeping into my mind that maybe, just maybe, my best judgment could also be used, and maybe it was beginning to sink in that Jesus Christ came for the people and not for the system symbolized by the chancery.

The chancery was the beginning of a three-year period during which I continually had to face adjusting to the church, letting it be or, if I didn't like working for the company, getting out. On the surface everything was fine: Roh was out there giving retreats to the nuns and telling them how fantastic this vow of chastity was. At $50 a crack this young hero would go out and have all the novices sit at his feet, hanging on every word. If *he* can believe it! I was defending the machine in public when people assaulted it, and in private spewing out my own frustration.

It was obvious at the chancery that I wasn't happy and I'm sure they knew I wasn't the loyal son they'd hoped I'd be, so they sent me to Hastings. I taught there and coached football and basketball for a year, and I found it as much therapy as anything. But for some reason I was causing a problem for the pastor, and after a year—without warning—I was transferred to another parish in Hastings. At the second parish I got more involved in a pastoral ministry, counseling and visiting, but I also found myself starting to lash out like an adolescent. In strange ways I was out to barb the bishop, to get back at the authority figure in my life. I grew a beard because I knew that would really get him and just did things for the sake of being different.

And so I lived until I went to the University of Notre Dame for a two-week seminar on personalism in education, two weeks of a close look at what teachers are about, how they exist as persons, how they live with themselves, what their aims are in school. It was two weeks of structured sensitivity, where you got a chance to go to the roots of what you really were and what was holding you back from becoming a complete functioning human being.

In the group sessions I think I came into touch with my powers, my talents, my masculinity—God, don't think that one wasn't in doubt—my weaknesses, the discovery that I could say I'm O.K. without bragging and realize I didn't need some external authority to tell me I was all right. I discovered for the first time in my life what truth means other than the Aristotelian equation of the mind with objective reality. I discovered truth as truth that involved the piece of transparency of oneself, and of the necessity to make a concerted effort to speak that truth, speak what is within a person rather than always checking to see if what you are saying conforms with what is expected by the institution that employs you, by the people whom you are serving. This seems strange for me to say, now thirty-three years old, but I had never trusted my own opinion; I had always deferred to a legal authority, a theological authority. My life had been dedicated to earning authority's approval. Then I discovered that I wasn't getting it any more and I was angry. You dirty people, you have me worried. Approve of me!

With that also came a real look into the whole business of celibacy. I was brought to face the games of different relationships. Why, when it boiled down, did I find I spent a lot of time with teenage girls? Did I really call Sister Mary Whatever to see how her new assignment was, and if so, why did I spend forty-five minutes on the phone and never ask her about her work? I grew a lot in those two weeks and I came to a point of saying, Your sexuality isn't always an evil thing. It's something you don't have to be worried about all the time, keeping up the guard-all shield.

So much was new. I became drunk "being honest." I acted out of my overenthusiasm and hurt some of my closest friends in ways I regret today. I met Corinne at Notre Dame and discovered for the first time as an adult a life in which I had someone near, personally close, with whom I could run through everything and through that person continually come into touch with myself and discover what was really there.

I went back to Nebraska and I lasted five weeks. I wanted to get back to Notre Dame to work for a Ph.D. in counseling, and also something within me had been touched by Corinne and other friends there. The bishop didn't want to give me permission to go, so for the first time in my church life I made a decision. I just went. My faculties were immediately suspended in my own diocese and the bishop made me promise not to say Mass, preach, or hear confessions in Lincoln, or else he would not write to South Bend for faculties there. Also, there was a scholarship that never came through, so I had to borrow money to stay at Notre Dame, money I'm still paying off today.

This was the fall of 1971, and as classes proceeded I spent more and more time with Corinne. I started counseling privately with a psychologist on the staff who started to make me face some pretty basic issues like sexuality and authority. I started to see the responsibility of making personal choices and living by them and I was feeling good about it. The shackles of the priesthood were off. I lived in a dorm and I wasn't Father Roh; I was Bob Roh, and I accepted myself more and more. I became in touch with my own feelings, affections, emotions. Before that I had separated myself from people because I was afraid I didn't know where my limits were, where I would stop.

The relationship with Corinne developed until I came to the point of saying, By damn, the next step is marriage. I couldn't keep bitching about the priesthood while living off the fat of it. Face what you are going to get as a priest; face that you are going to be part of an institution. Face where you are as a priest, where you are with God. Stop using the institution and stop using this woman as a way of sliding through life.

I needed time to sit back and think about it, to pray about it, and I couldn't do it there at Notre Dame. I wouldn't have trusted the decision. I called the bishop and asked to come back to Lincoln. To him, my coming back meant I was set in the priesthood. Most people here think that I'm in for good now. Even priest friends feel I'm in solid. But I'm in a terrible state of ambivalence, a state you can't keep yourself in for long, because you become ineffective. Right now I'm operating on a timetable of about six months. At the end of that time I'll have made my decision.

If I leave it will be because I have made the choice between two goods—priesthood and marriage. I never had the framework to make that decision before, because all there was was existential celibacy and theoretical marriage. I don't feel the need to stay away from people any more; the guard-all shield is shattered. I have come out of my post-adolescent syndrome and I must make an adult decision. But I'm still a boy with a toothache who's taking time to see if it should be drilled and filled or yanked out. There is going to be some dying either way. I'm slowly learning that I can't have my cake and eat it, that every choice closes off certain options.

I'd stay because I see the priest as a person in a group of people relating to God, a person who says something to the people about a hope Jesus gives them, that he came for them. I am learning to keep that message separate from the institutional, cultural, and historical realities in the church. I'm spending a lot of time visiting house to house, trying to get people to share at a gut level what affects them in life, trying to gather them around the Eucharist table. I want to be available to people, to help them work through their birth control problems, divorce problems.

Then there is the side of me that wants to get out and say screw the whole thing. Another brick is coming out and that is the best contribution I can make, to help destroy a non-lifegiving system. Another and another and the whole thing crumbles to the ground and we start from scratch.

If I take a quiet moment I can list most of the things that have brought me to this critical point in my priesthood. First, I feel wasted; I have thoughts, contributions, but because of my superiors' preconceived ideas they will not even consider them. Second, I am living in an unreal world held together by codes and laws, a world in which ignorance is the best tool for keeping it together. Third, it is a world where priests who are preaching God's word can't trust one another, can't pray with one another, have no desire to pray together unless the ritual of the day demands it. Fourth, I have experienced love, not love of my role but love of me with all the imperfections I have. Fifth, when I got away from my role as priest and could function as a normal human being I felt better than I had for years. I woke up each morning without that feeling of five onionskins being over me. Sixth, I have come to grips with the fact that all women are not enticing me, that I don't have to have an electric fence around me.

I could talk theory, about what I'd do if I left. I would work as a dedicated layman, as a marriage counselor or social worker in the middle of Chicago. But administration and bureaucracy would still face me there; I know that.

I sit here an overwhelmed man because I have experienced a

love that wants to reach out and embrace and smother, yet a love that draws back and allows me to make a decision. I can tell about the five buckets of tears spread between South Bend and here and just a lot of sobering thought. If you've experienced love like that and you decide to stay in, you're not going to do it for anything you don't consider very, very worthwhile. I've paid too much to be back here to worry about whether I wear a collar or not walking down the street. I often fight people calling me "Father" now. I don't want that identity. I was an inch from being married, from possibly becoming a true father, and I don't like hearing the word when its use shoves me into a caste, apart, off from people.

I've never been in such pain, but I've never felt as free. Up in the pulpit I'll say what I want, no nambsy-pambsy worrying about who isn't going to like this, or if the other priests approve of me. I find I pray an awful lot, I spill out the depths of my soul to God now. I don't think I ever celebrate Mass or kneel down that I don't think about what I'm trying to come to grips with.

The priest is supposed to be the man up there with all the answers, and here is one going through a deeper crisis than most of the people who look to him for stability. But in these pains I come to the point where most people are at, and I can relate to the kind of faith and hope I tell them to have. Until you are broke, until you miss a woman's touch, you shouldn't be talking to a man who just lost his wife or a divorced woman trying to put her life together.

[SIX MONTHS LATER BOB ROH HAD MADE HIS DECISION.]

There was no sudden decision. It was a slow, painful growing up, looking inside, a lot of gray. I was very free to live and be myself here in Brainard with two ideal priests who let me be and yet offered themselves for cooperation and for work.

To pinpoint the time when I said I would stay in is difficult. Symbolically it came when I communicated with Notre Dame that I wasn't coming back for the program and at the Holy Thursday Chrism Mass at the Cathedral.

I guess I felt a little bit like Jonah, who tried to run away, a little bit like Moses; and a lot of the call back to the priesthood isn't something I can conceptualize and present in a beautiful statement. It's just that He has something for me to do. It's that feeling of call. I need to be in the ministry to answer something that is real in me. At the same time I still would like to be married, to have my own family. But as I sit here today I can live without marriage more easily than I can live without the ministry.

I made the decision to remain when I decided that my faith in Christ, in his spirit, really was very important to me, that I did feel the need to say something on behalf of Christ. I see the priesthood as a tremendous opportunity to serve people. As a Catholic I know of no other way of doing those things that are most important to me.

Other things about clericalism and the church have become clearer. I think I am a little more comfortable with the Roman collar than I was in April. It isn't a big deal for me right now, and I find that if I am working with a group of people who find it important, I can put it on. But I can also take it off as easily when I work with a group of kids. I find that the world is changing too, that more and more people can use the word "Father" as a title and not as a paternalistic pedestal.

I spent the past years bitching about the church; so why am I embracing it, and what changes can I hope to make? First, I have discovered that the church is not the chancery office. The church is not in the canon law book. The church is in the people trying to come together, overcome their own frustrations and anxieties. And they want a leader. It is really important now that people accept your priesthood because of who you are, not just your office. The priest must be authentic. I will call people to serve, and I find myself very comfortable in taking advantage of the priest's role that has been created by long tradition. I can take that and work from it, remembering, of course, my own responsibility to that tradition. At the moment I can stay away from church politics and reform of the governing structures of the church.

I am not entirely proud of this position; I think it could be a real copout. I think a man has to eventually get involved in the politics of the church if we are to have significant reform. I can't lull myself into thinking that Brainard, Nebraska, is where I should spend my life. It would be easy and comfortable to do that, to live as a country gentleman.

The most important item I came to grips with in these months was authority and how I was going to react to it or live with it. I acknowledged that I was very dependent on authority, eager to win the approval of others, and I did it very well and won a lot of trophies. I'm now beginning to be comfortable when authorities are looking askance at me; the church does not have to pat me on the back for what I'm doing. I am beginning to learn to look at the issue and the success of the issue itself rather than see how it comes out in the approval-disapproval register at the chancery office.

Along the way I considered many possibilities, one was to leave the Catholic Church and become a Lutheran minister, where I could be married and still serve. I have a great feeling for the Lutheran tradition, but I still have a more intense feeling for the Catholic world and I must work in reforming it.

I am fully aware of the call I have and the responsibility to listen to it and allow it to rise to the surface to take its proper importance. By admitting that and acting on it I am aware of the hurt I caused friends; I'm aware of the commitment Corinne had to me and I don't feel good about it. When I made my decision she shared with me in a marvelous way her own hurt, her own love for me, and yet a complete appreciation of the choice. Her arrival in my life was one of those God-sent blessings; nobody else could have done for me what she did.

I couldn't say that I am choosing celibacy for life by my decision. It's only for as long as the church requires it. I think it's an injustice, but as long as I need to be celibate to be a priest, I will be celibate. But that celibacy is dependent upon a continual grace, a continual call, continual awareness that priesthood is meaningful in my sight, in men's sight, and, above all, in God's sight. I think this requires a lot of praying.

If it were possible to go back in time and I had the choice to relive the last eighteen months, I hope I would make the same choices. It brought me to a point where I can be much more honest about decisions in my life. I teach differently; I'm different with people. I'm much more self-confident, secure; I don't have to put on a lot of masks. I can live with people who can accept me and live with people who find my opinions and my way of living distasteful and uncomfortable. I can be very happy with myself, and a lot of that came from being loved in a time of crisis by people who made me feel accepted and who taught me that—maybe—that is what God and faith are all about.

"Father Bill"

Until he begins to talk, he looks like a man completely in possession of himself, secure, confident—a priest whom life has treated well. In his forties, he is handsome, with a trim muscular body that has a marked waistline where most men his age would settle for a gentle indentation. His voice is surprisingly low for a man with such strong features, such burning eyes, such a jutting chin.

Call him "Father Bill," for his real name can't be used. If his real name were attached to his story the vocation that he has struggled to maintain would be put in jeopardy.

He is a man who rarely frowns as he talks, yet his smiles are not easily mustered. He has the face of a struggling physics student who is looking at a complicated problem on a blackboard, trying to take it apart so that he can solve it piece by piece. He frowns when it appears he hasn't the ability to solve the problem.

He comes from a family that was so emotionally cold and severe that he and his brothers and sisters couldn't wait to leave home. He escaped to the warm bosom of Holy Mother Church, which had offered him some solace in his lonely life. Other seminarians complained of the life, but "Father Bill" loved it. He readily slept on the floor to mortify his senses, he attended devotions slavishly.

All the while he felt basically unworthy of the priesthood, so when ordination day came and family and friends wanted to kiss the hand of the new priest, he could hardly believe the hand was his.

He was popular in his first parish, too popular, it turned out, for his bishop to accept, so he was sent to another parish to live under a dictator of a pastor. Frustrated but still sure about his priesthood, he went to Florida for a vacation and, for the first time in his life, danced with a girl. Feeling tainted and far too human to be a priest, he confided to a psychologist friend that he was worried—he enjoyed a woman's touch.

On the surface he remained serene. After many successful years as pastor of a church in a smaller city, he asked to go to the inner city, where he felt the real witness was to be made. His reward: beatings and rejection for his stands. Although he was beginning to sense that he had some worth outside of the priestly role—which also frightened him and seemed to threaten his vocation—there was no one to share himself with. Finally, on the verge of a nervous breakdown, he found someone, a nun about to leave her order. He broke down and she comforted him. Then followed a fairy-tale week together when he abandoned himself, finding a new worth in himself, a new acceptance; but he was torn between the call—fainter now—and a woman. He went back to his parish and found his answer there.

I was that "afterthought" child in a large family, the last before twin beds were brought in. But for all intents and purposes I was an only child, because the next eldest was many years older than me. My dad was a strange man, a sort of Prussian type. The children had no communication whatsoever with the man. He just sat at the head of the table at dinner and nobody uttered a word. In fact, the first time I remember talking to him was when I was twelve. Perhaps it's an interesting pattern. As I look back, we kids left home as early as possible, some into religious life and one of us literally kicked out of the house because he was going with a Protestant.

Dad never got out of grade school, but he was an intelligent, aware person. He was a proud man, a strong man, and even my mother was scared to death of him. He was never physical with her. Silence was the control. We never went on relief in our home town—let's call it Boston*—during the Depression, although we surely were eligible. He was just too proud to do that.

Nothing was ever said at home about my going into the seminary. If anything, the push came from the nuns of the parish, who saw me as that kid who always served Mass. To me this was the greatest thing I could do. The nuns. I guess they were as naïve as I was about life. Not too many years ago I got this panic call from one of the sisters I had gotten to know over the years. She had suffered for eighteen years with a series of internal lesions and nobody in the convent ever took it too seriously. You're really not sick; what the hell, you teach today, they'd say. And she did, eight and ten hours a day. She was going through the change of life, and she didn't have the slightest idea what it was all about. She cried. How do babies come? She hadn't a clue. For some reason she thought she was pregnant.

We lived fairly close to the church, so I was always in its shadow —actually and psychologically. It was the eternal womb to me. This was a place where I could find strength and where I could fantasize totally, fantasize that I was somehow understood by this church. I don't think this was unusual in my era. The high-priest cultic role impressed me. All those processions and silk and gold, and the admired priest who was the center of it all.

Right after grade school, not knowing really why or what or anything, I was off to the minor seminary. I had come from a background that was so emotionally bankrupt I was eager for this

* Certain details have been changed to preserve anonymity.

dream world that the priesthood would be. Something finally to depend on. While other guys kicked and screamed about rules and regulations, to me it was something reliable, the structure upheld me. I had no concept of me as a person. I had to be a priest, and if this was what was needed let's get on with it. Up before six each morning, a morning Mass, then a thanksgiving Mass before breakfast, noontime when I'd go to the chapel and examine my conscience or my miserable state of unworthiness and how I had sinned since noon the day before.

No talking above the first floor, assigned places in chapel, study hall, prayer hall. And particular friendships were certainly taboo. Couldn't walk with the same person twice. But that all reinforced my very strict background. Rules were to be followed and not questioned. If there was any difficulty in those days, it wasn't about my vocation. I must have had one or I wouldn't have been there, and the guys who left were "spoiled priests." I honestly admit some of that lingers with me today about men that leave, although it's growing less. I was the perfect seminarian. With such a lack of confidence in self, I was perfect. And the security—I loved the security of the seminary and what the priesthood eventually would bring.

I was an athletic kid, a pretty good football player. I must have been in the major seminary when I got a chance to play on the pickup team of local guys who went up against a semi-pro team. Word of that got back to the seminary and I was mortified. There, I had broken a rule, brought disgrace to the seminary, shame upon the notion of priesthood. I guess there must have been girls on the sidelines and that was even a greater sin. Anyhow, that was reason for expulsion. I was so guilty I felt the rector had the right to do it. The rules counted; personal responsibility: zero. Reflecting on girls, I recall that I must have been horsing around with some girl late in grade school and it got reported back home. My dad whaled the hell out of me. That was our first real communication.

I fantasized about girls, but I never followed through. No self-assurance, no self-confidence. I had the wishes, desires to be with girls, but I wouldn't let them get inside the circle we were taught to live within. And to do anything with girls would involve leaving the womb of the church. The church was my girl, she could provide all the things I needed. I was convinced I didn't have any sexuality. Everybody knows priests are asexual.

By the time of my ordination I had mastered the art of selective amnesia, call it sublimation, call it what you will. I had questions about what I was into, but I never faced them. I had a question about this vow of celibacy, but hadn't a clue to the reality. There must be something in this, because they're asking me to give it up, but I left it at that. Normal pubescent sexual experience? None. I did not have a conscious erection until I was thirty-two years old. Let's put that in context and get a little Freudian about it. My sexual relationship was almost totally maternal—the church. Therefore, any notions of aggressiveness in it would be forbidden. The Great Sin was simply sexuality, and especially when you vow celibacy.

As I approached ordination I was of the old spirituality and had a certain fear of any kind of human expression. I'm not knocking that kind of spirituality, because historically that's where everybody was. But it said, I am a worm, I'm worthless, I am of little value. My only value comes from the fact of my God and what I can do for Him. Human intimacy had no place; feelings had no place. Avoid them like the plague. And all the while somewhere in the back of my head were the questions. I didn't want to ask them, because I might come up with another question: Do I really want this? Do I really want to be a priest? I can honestly say I never confronted myself with those questions before ordination. Even to question was to be disloyal.

The first Mass was at my home parish three days after ordination, and it was beautiful. Church filled. I blessed everybody in sight with reckless abandon. All the while thinking, though, This ain't me. This couldn't be me, the person whose hand they wanted to kiss. I guess I was about 20 per cent there that day.

By the time I was assigned to my first parish in a tiny town in upstate Massachusetts I was starting, in a small way, to get back at the authority that had suppressed me so. I took a great interest in the avant-garde liturgical movements, Catholic Action movements of the day. You have to remember that Catholic Action was the underground church of that day, this whole notion of lay people having a role in the working of the church was an inroad of great vision for the future. I fell in love with liturgy. It was my first real expression of emotion. I loved the notion of music, of flowing vestments rather than the fiddleback chasubles, good Gregorian chants. I read all the books on liturgical reform I could get my hands on.

Through all this I was beginning to squeak: I matter. Here I am. Christ, I do make a difference. As I look back, I was trying so hard to find some way to express myself, my person, me.

My first pastor was older, Italian, and benign—you don't find that combination too often. I was outgoing, up on liturgy, good with the kids, and he let me run with the ball. I tried to be a paternal figure, but one who talked sort of like Bing Crosby—maybe the kind of person I wanted to talk to when I was a kid. No days off, ablaze giving instructions, taking kids off somewhere, coaching. Sort of living out my own adolescence.

The kids came to me—knocked down the door—with their problems, and I didn't have a clue as to what they were talking about. Masturbation? Sure, that was in the book, and it was a mortal sin —I could tell them that. I had as much as any other priest: the absolute answer to any question. But no personal experiences, nothing from real life. Again, I was a priest and I was different. I walked on water. But I think I was good with the kids; I wasn't punitive. I'd seen too much of that. Then I got involved in parole work and a whole list of stuff. Jesus Christ Superstar, here he was. And what did I need for refueling to keep going? Nothing, I thought, and I believed. I was a priest and that was enough.

In the parish everything was going fine. Down at the chancery, not so fine. I got some kind of an award one year, and that kind of publicity didn't sit well. I was called in, and for the first time I really was violent with an authority figure. Why did he have to bring me down for this? How was I hurting the church? And that was a signal to him. Too popular, too successful. What I needed was a strict pastor to knock me into shape.

So I was transferred and got a new pastor. He was a bastard, an old-school tyrant. Suit or cassock and collar at dinner. Stand until grace was over. Listen to the radio during the meal. No conversation unless he initiated it. I'd be in my room and get a buzz: "Go downstairs and get my glasses."

On the surface, as always, I had complete control. I had that in the sem; most people think I still have it today. But inside—seething, ready to lop his head off, and feeling very guilty about it and uncharitable. We had to be in by ten each night, and nothing was done without his approval. But by this time I was becoming an angry young man. I would make rather powerful statements about how people had to get involved in the church to make it work. At the next opportunity the pastor refuted everything I had said.

I was instrumental in getting people to participate in Latin and to do a minimal amount of singing. But the pastor never acknowledged any of it. He ignored it: a spitting image of my dad. It was during those times that I really had my first consciousness of personal sexuality in the sense of erection, emission. I finally had gone into combat against Mother Church and somehow that started liberating me. I know a psychiatrist could do a chapter on all that entails.

A priest friend and I took a bus trip down to Key West. We went to a night club—really mild stuff by today's standards—and I danced with one of the cabaret girls, the first time I had ever danced in my life. It scared me out of my mind. Sodom and Gomorrah. I was waiting for the flood to come and looking for the highest peak so I could sit there and hope like hell it would stop raining. I hadn't done a thing down there, honest to God. But I fantasized I had gone completely wild, that I had done something hideously wrong. Guilty, wow, was I guilty!

I knew something was there, some can of worms I didn't want to take the lid off, because then, well—the worms would come out. My priesthood would be threatened. I was ready to be destroyed, I just knew it. So I went to a doctor, hoping that he could explain all this to me. You have to understand that my view was that a vocation exempted me from human feelings, from liking the touch of a woman or the smell of her. The doctor told me the facts of life, that my body was put together like any other man's and I would have the same responses. And I thought to myself, If you're just like other guys, then you can't be a priest. Honest. I was unfaithful to my vows. There was a whole mystique I had about the priesthood. I was looked on as a devotional guy in the seminary. I would sleep on the floor, I could spend an entire night in chapel. Mortify those senses! But now, what was going on?

I was utterly convinced that what was awakening in me was abnormal. And there was this tough pastor who didn't help either. This might be an example: The kids had a basketball tournament and they asked me to act as the master of ceremonies—make a few jokes and hand out the trophies. I didn't fight it off too hard. The pastor walked in while I was on and walked right back out again. The next morning at nine the buzzer rang. "Come to my room," he said, sounding as somber as he could. He closed the door, we sat down, and he started in. "You are an unworthy priest. You don't like me, don't like my parish. As of now you will be no part of this church, and I want you out of my house by six tonight."

I went back to my room. Had I been unpriestly? No. Really unworthy? No. I was scared to death, but he forced me to ask myself those questions which pushed me to an increased but still lukewarm awareness. I wasn't going to kiss his ass, but I also couldn't get angry. I wasn't at that point yet where I could really go at him. He wasn't the church, but he was the tie with the church and I wasn't going to cut that. I went back and said, "I was sent here. I'm staying here. If you want to change me, you write the chancery." He just looked at me. "You'll say no Mass in this church, you will not preach, you will take no part in the activities of my church."

I got in my car and drove and came back late that night. Same thing the next day, just drove and slept in the car. I couldn't really share this with anybody, and that was a problem; it was impossible for me to be intimate about anything back then. I'm sure my classmates were going through some similar things. But again, if you're a priest you're not weak and you don't show it. On the second night I came back and found a schedule under my door giving me back all the things I had before, except that I could not preach at Mass. So, basically, he had capitulated. People noticed I wasn't preaching, and I gave some excuse and just lived through that until I was transferred. Three years in the parish and all that crap. But still I had no thoughts about leaving the priesthood.

I finally got my first church as pastor in a little rural place eighty miles outside Boston. It was like reliving the first parish all over again, except this time I was pastor. I was big on liturgical reform, and I was busy working with the adult groups, the kids, anybody, everybody. There was work to be done, but the one item that was missing throughout was that things were happening. But I wasn't happening. I was still behind the Roman collar, and I knew that role down to the teeth, what to do, how to react. Vatican II had happened and the liturgy was blown wide open—the very things I'd worked for—the church was being liberated.

And I was still the same old me: role-playing the priest.

I was asking people to be different, to be transformed into feeling humans. Participate in the Mass, open up. But I wasn't demanding of myself. This whole business of my sexuality. I had had a taste of my first sexual awareness, and I didn't know what to do with it. I resolved it for the most part by the ancient means: walking the floors, cold showers, praying the Rosary interminably.

Those were lonely days, but I convinced myself I could weather that. I was used to being lonely. I had good friends there in the parish, but never would they know that Father was hurting. Then something must have started happening and it wasn't that I wanted anything to happen; I wanted to stay in that priestly role, period. Because if I didn't I'd have to face a lot of things that mortal man has to face, then I would have to be responsible and make decisions, choices. I sensed I'd have to, for the first time, really decide if I wanted to be a priest.

But I pushed all the questions into the background and continued my adolescence. I enjoyed people, sports, preaching, counseling. Did everything but look at myself. Then I started counseling at a local public school, and while I enjoyed it, I was scared. There the priestly role didn't mean anything. I was on a secular payroll, being able to pay for a car, to pay off the seminary tuition. What I found at the school frightened me: acceptance for what I was doing. I wasn't used to that. I viewed my acceptance in the church as coming just because I was a priest. I went up the salary scale quickly and I found I liked that. I pinpoint this because it was the first time I saw I could have some value outside the ordinary functions of a priest, and I didn't know where or if to go somewhere with it. That was what frightened me. I keep on saying frightened, yes, I guess it was exactly that. I was frightened of myself, of successes.

About this time I was really starting to get the apostolic itch, and minority groups seemed to be where it was at. Besides that, the rural church made me restless. It wasn't enough challenge any more, now that I was getting some sense of myself and that I was worth something. I asked the chancery for a ghetto parish and they assigned me to a parish that still had a largely white congregation but was in an area quickly turning into a brown ghetto, mainly Cubans and Puerto Ricans. I was going to ride in on my white charger and blow this place apart. I had never had contact with minority groups, didn't know the first thing about them, but they had love, didn't they? They were people, weren't they? I was a priest. Instant salvation coming up!

I was naïve, but I wasn't so naïve as not to know I was going to need a lot of support from the chancery. A lot of the work would be extraparochial, and I would need their backing and some money. Most of all I wanted understanding, understanding in the sense of: If there's a little question, damn it, we're still with you even though the work is different and we don't know exactly what you're doing. I would be in community affairs and they had to be ready to stand up for me. I might be doing things that wouldn't look like they were part of the church, but they had to bear with me.

With the civil rights movement came the first real blowouts. My white parishioners were going crazy, right in the middle of all this, and I wasn't resting too easy either. I got roughed up in the riots, beat up once trying to keep the lid on. Then three Chicanos were jailed on phony charges, the police just wanted to have somebody in jail. So I supported them and they eventually got out. Then the letters and calls came in. I couldn't accept it, because they hit me where it really hurt. Some were calling me an unworthy priest. It frightened me; conflict wasn't my bag. I found myself disengaging further from what was church and getting into what was the real world. I started talking about consciousness and accountability, which incidentally might have been fine out in the country, but this church had a handful of minority members and the whites didn't want to hear about equality, because that meant that spic right down the block.

Here I was in my prophetic role, and people started resigning from the parish. Massive rejection was all I could see. And before that I was Bing Crosby. Everybody loved me. I paced the room at night: Why can't they accept the truth? I have it. Just listen. This was where my first doubts about the effectiveness of the church in dealing with minority groups really cropped up.

On the surface, cool. Inside, Vesuvius. On the surface, coping with the situation; I knew what needed to be said. Inside, five miles back emotionally. The seminary had reinforced my early training beautifully. When there was conflict I was the cool one. I had no emotions. I was still the priest. But at night I'd walk the floor, walk the walls.

I got continuing static from the parishioners as I moved along. From September to June the parish was church. In summer it was a community center for the minority kids. And the whites resented this bitterly—the way the building started looking, the hundreds of dollars to replace broken windows. It was their church and these low-lifes were working it over. Their support began falling off, so I wrote, begged, pleaded with the chancery for the money they'd promised. Nothing. Not even answers to my letters.

By the end of the year I was a wreck, an emotional wreck. The one guy who got me that far was a Cuban psychiatrist who would just sit down, alternately asking me tough questions about what I was doing and giving me massive doses of support. I didn't have enough sense to say, Look, I'm falling apart. I need some time away. Hell, no! I just launched into the next program.

I had known a nun on and off for a long time and she was having some doubts too about where the church should be moving. She told me she'd asked for a transfer to the inner city. I went to visit her and said, "You don't know what you're getting into." There was really no reason for me to tell her that, but there was something there—always had been—and I had refused to face it. I was above all that. But my mask was slipping. What that trip meant was: Hey, I need somebody.

I wanted somebody so bad I could taste it. Not in the carnal sense. Just somebody to care for me, about me. She felt that right away, and I knew she did, and all kinds of walls caved in. That's the first time I remember crying, just sobbing. And just being held by a woman who was compassionate enough to reach out to a drowning man! And she's a pretty girl, beautiful, and I'm grateful as hell for her. She just held me, that was it. But, oh, for the first time. It was a beautiful thing. The rational man that was me dissolved right before her eyes.

She suddenly became aware of the chink in my armor. She was having deep doubts about staying in too. Suddenly she could see there might be something there between us. I came away wondering, Maybe this is the way to go. Maybe this is the real me. I was shared for the first time; emotions started to have an effect on the way I acted. I still had control, but it was slipping. There was that awareness: This is a possibility.

I shared this with the psychiatrist, and he said, "We can work together but somebody has to counsel with you and you have some problems to be talked out." So he sent me to a psychologist. I knew I had so many things to work out. The light was being put on those dark corners, but I didn't know if I wanted to look or not.

But I would no more openly admit that I needed help than the man in the moon. If you want to see a stubborn man at work: I went to that psychologist for two months, sixteen sessions of one hour each, before I said the first word. Going through hell inside but thinking, A priest doesn't do this. He's different. There was a fear of saying something that would bring disgrace upon me, upon the priesthood. Everything was up in the air, the possibility of leaving the priesthood, marrying the nun, checking out of a church that wasn't meeting people's needs.

Finally I opened up and it started pouring out—everything. My sexual repression, home life, priest myths, everything, which of course doesn't make you feel better right away. Only more confused. But to this day the assistant that lived with me doesn't know

I went through two years of therapy. My front was beautifully serene.

I was hurting so badly and couldn't find any release. Therapy didn't do it; the womb wasn't soothing me any more. So I went up to Canada to see the nun.

It was the idyllic, fairy-tale week together. Time ceased. No past, no future. Just me and her. God, it was beautiful. Something out of time and space. Well, how do you fall in love gracefully? And a priest with a nun? We were like two teenagers. We just wanted to be with each other every minute. Just to be able to reach out and touch the other person at any moment.

She had already decided before that week that she was going to leave her order, and today I sit here wondering why the hell I didn't go too. I really do. Why I didn't just stay there with her. Because when I came back I was hurting so badly for her. I really knew what hurt was all about.

All this time I was one of those people nuns and priests who were thinking of leaving felt comfortable with. I was a good listener, somebody who appeared to be feeling where things were at. I played the role perfectly. Here they were, holding up a mirror to the very things I was going through. I was sympathetic with them, I know that, and on the inside my stomach was doing somersaults.

After the week with that wonderful woman I went back to therapy with a new gusto. I was beginning to say I didn't have to be a priest, and then finally I could believe it. My total value was not in being a priest, it was in being me. I didn't have to stay in. I didn't have to stay in. I was trying desperately to build bridges, to get out of this damn priesthood, to get out of this damn church, to get away from the eternal tit. And every time I'd come to a dead end. I was offered a job as an administrator of a home for delinquent kids. It was all there, and yet the bridge always came to a dead end.

Why dead ends? Because I found I really wanted to be a priest. I couldn't be anything else. I tried to build those bridges, I tried.

But after you are touched you find you can begin to touch others. I had a whole new sensitivity to what the kids were going through, what married couples contended with. Real relationships. I could put the book aside and talk from the gut to them. And working this all through in therapy, realizing that I did not have to be a priest, confirmed that I must be one. Confusing? I realized the priesthood had meaning, I could bring meaning into other people's lives. And if I wouldn't be here, who the hell else would be?

I had a foot in both camps and that wasn't fair. I felt like a rat entering into this intimacy, then saying, No, I've got to think about it. Hold off. By this time the nun had already left her order and I had to do something. Here you have a man who was so down, dissatisfied, discouraged, disenchanted with the church, and a woman who rescued him. I was disenchanted with myself, but I was coming to grips with that, that I was a worthwhile person. I flew up to see her a few times, but I knew I could do a lot of damage to a person I loved by playing both sides.

The struggle in the parish continued, but the beauty of it was that I could feel, I could deal with these problems in a whole new way. I could feel what people were angry, happy, dissatisfied, hopeful about. She opened me up to that. And that was the worst summer in the city, with fights and killings and burnings.

Soon after, a good friend of mine was shot in his home. A wonderful man who had worked on so many projects with me. Dead! And the police weren't hunting too hard for suspects. That brought it all together for me.

I hit bottom. But I realized the church, a changing church, can respond, has to respond, has to be there. I had to be there. All this while, I was being kicked out of rectories when I asked for money for my projects. There were tremendous feelings of isolation from the church, alienation. But I found things improving because of my own input. I could do something on my own. The church was lagging behind, but it would catch up.

There was no dramatic moment when I said, Yes, I'm staying

in. Just a gradual realization of the worth of priesthood, a real love for it. But there was another love that had to be dealt with. If celibacy were optional, I'd have exercised that option. We came as close as you can get to an understanding about why I had to stay, but for at least a year afterwards I wondered if I'd done right. I still wonder. She is still unmarried, and I think we could make a great couple.

I had been in the inner city five years and I knew that was enough for me. So when I was offered a place on the outskirts of the city I said yes. By the time I left, there were a good number of minority families in the church, and because of the fact that I was white and they were brown and proud of it, they didn't make a big deal of my leaving. We'd suffered through threatened bombings of the church center, and they knew me and I knew them. There was no need for any big thing about my leaving. One Puerto Rican guy—you know, house full of kids, married a couple of times, a beautiful guy—and his wife had me over for dinner. And he set down this bottle of vermouth, a fifth of Gilbey's gin and just looked at me. So we started in, and we finished both of those, a bottle of wine, and a six-pack of beer. "How about arm wrestling?" he said about midnight. "O.K. you bastard," I said, and I threw him over, and he jumped up and hugged me. "You honky priest." Acceptance. A hell of a way, but that was acceptance.

After going through a period of doubt, people might wonder if I'm secure today about my priesthood. Not at all, and that's the beauty of it. I'm no more secure than anybody in their job. I'm weak, the church is inadequate, but we both have value. The church will become more human or it will die. The same for my priesthood. My own strength is that I can now speak to people where they are, wondering, doubtful—because that's me. I've gone through it. My strength is that I'm weak. Where I am now, we can respond to Vatican II, try new liturgies, accept responsibilities.

I don't think any bishop, pope, or pastor could drive me out of the church now. I know what I want to do and I'll do it, and they can go ahead and do their thing too. I still love the cultic part of the priesthood—Mass, sacraments, counseling, teaching. I'm part of that. One of the great needs of society, the world, still comes down to people needing, craving faith, hope, and love. I think the church has a corner on that market.

It's not that all problems are solved with me. But certainly I know that I don't want to hurt another woman. If I see anything cropping up I really watch that. And I pray like crazy now, not the breviary—that turns me off—but real talking to God. All that prayer, if you don't know your own head, won't help. That's why the two years in therapy were prayer to me. I guess I can get through days now and not seek the warmth of a woman, because I can pray, I can cry, I can feel.

Through my growth in the face of massive repression, I feel that celibacy wasn't the key issue. I had to grow to maturity. Celibacy surely may continue to be an issue for me, for after all, priests are not that different. Celibacy is still a viable life style, and right now I opt for it. I opt for the priesthood.

"Father Jerome Killeen"

This man, whom we'll call "Father Jerome Killeen," is not exactly the kind to turn a woman's head. He is of average height, drinks a trifle more than he should, has the paunch of an inactive middle-aged man, and somehow the flaccid skin on his face gives the impression it has been used before—like gift wrapping paper the second time around.

"Father Killeen" sits in a small rectory on the West Coast, spending some months there before he leaves for South America and missionary work in a mountainous rural area. He tells about his life and priesthood, the ups and downs, with little show of emotion on his face. Yet his life is quite different from what a person might expect from a Roman Catholic priest. In simple words, "Father Killeen" has yielded to the flesh. Yielded many, many times.

Born in the Midwest of solid Irish Catholic stock, he entered the seminary of a missionary-oriented order after high school and was ordained nine years later. A good boy became a good seminarian who became a good priest. But slowly he began to realize that the simplistic forms of goodness that had been taught to him as supreme values were no longer enough. Immersed in the cauldron of civil and workers' rights in the South, he soon found that he had to do a total renovation job on a model that was out of date and becoming useless in the 1960s.

He stayed in the South for ten years and discovered through his work the power of the spirit that the Gospel talks about, that priests preach about, but so few people internalize. He found he could stand up against injustice and win. And he found that he could lie down alongside a woman and participate in the most human of all acts.

But, at a time when his sex life seemed to be in tune with his priesthood, it happened. The woman he was having an affair with missed her period. She missed a second month. And his priesthood slipped further away as each day passed.

Bless me, Father, for I have sinned in the church's eyes. I have quite a few things that I've never confessed before. I am unmarried and yet I have indulged in sexual intercourse. Many times, Father. I've had affairs with different women. Oh, and by the way, Father, I'm a Roman Catholic priest.

Maybe that is a good introduction for anyone who would be scandalized by what follows. But perhaps people are more understanding. And I'd have to add to the end of that confession: By the way, Father, I'm not sorry or guilty about anything that ever happened with any of the women.

Let's call the city Mobile*—although that's not it—where I was assigned for the first ten years of my priesthood. I lived in a parish, taught religion at a high school and worked out of a social center. I came to Mobile as a typical seminary product, naïve but at least literate. The seminary kept you in a continuing state of anticipation of a life that was to be more or less tranquil, where you were to experience happiness and more or less enjoy it. Faith was on our

* Certain details have been changed to preserve anonymity.

side and we could prove that from the Council of Trent, and so it was an angelic frame of reference—one where life seemingly would present no great problems or conflicts. I was so naïve! So naïve that when a cop pulled me over for doing eighty miles an hour I couldn't quite grasp I had done something wrong. I was a child of God, nothing could hurt me, and I was to go to Mobile and make as many converts as I could, to be a sort of religious colonialist. I could bring civilization and religion to all the people.

It turned out to be quite different. But I don't want to fault the seminary for anything. They did the best they could. They taught me about books and rituals and history. But a seminary can't humanize a person; that can only happen in real life. You must cooperate with the gift of humanity that is extended to you in the real world. Some choose not to accept.

The early years in Mobile were years of shedding skins and learning that I didn't have as much to offer blacks or anybody as they had to offer me. The people taught me the world isn't as programmed as I thought it was, that we can't judge people by a certain act. For example, truancy doesn't always mean a kid doesn't care about education. Non-support doesn't always mean a man doesn't care about his children. Violence doesn't always mean that a person is homicidal. Now these are on the negative side, but they're drawn from a popular stereotype of ghetto populations.

Blacks are more expressive in their feelings and less hypocritical. They don't have norms to protect that somebody else gave them. They can be clearer, more honest, have greater integrity. I often link the black struggle for identity with my people, the Irish; many of the parallels are there, but unfortunately too many turned into Lace Curtain Irish who forgot their past.

It was a black woman who taught me about love. I had an affair with her for six years, and I learned to share the intimacies of her life, to go through the sufferings and joys that any normal person goes through as they seek to find a spirit of humanity. I would be fearful about talking about myself now had it not been for that woman and other women in my life. They made me whole.

I was thirty before I had my first sexual experience; before that there were some mild flirtations. Some might question, Well, isn't that a violation of your oath? You vowed to be celibate. I am celibate; I am not married. But I think celibacy is more than that; chastity is more than that. Chastity ought to mean a type of innocence in dealing with other people whereby you're willing to take chances with them.

When it happened, sex was more of an amazement to me than anything else. I certainly did examine myself after I began to get involved with women, to find out what I was doing, but I don't ever remember guilt being an ingredient. I found I couldn't go along with the church on the teaching about sex outside of marriage being such a hideous thing. It was beautiful. No one was being harmed in the process, so how could it be wrong? Sinful? Surely war is more sinful and a condemnation of war by the church was hard to get.

I think if any person does it simply for sexual gratification, then he or she is prostituting powers of procreation. But if it's a case of two consenting adults performing a sexual act for which they are willing to take the responsibility, and the motivation is one of intimate love, then they don't have to apologize to anybody for it. God is love!

Let me talk a little about my work in the South and how sex came into the picture, and maybe the kind of life I led will come through clearer. I always felt I had a call to be a priest even as a young boy. I felt it in my work in the South; I feel it now. But the feeling of call is more individuated now. As a child I had a general, vague, superhuman idea of being a priest, but now it's being myself as a priest, a part but not all of my personality. I am an individual who will be a priest forever. It's something I carry with me and will always carry with me even if someday people tried to force me to leave the kind of priesthood the church has outlined. I hope that won't happen. I expect to be in the *Kennedy Directory* every year; I hope to be in the necrology later on, but not too soon.

The priesthood is my life blood. Still I can't say that I go along with everything that some medieval monk has written or that the Curia declares. It is a unique expression. And over the fifteen years of my priesthood I've found great power. I think there is something to the idea of the Spirit motivating people. I think it's a spiritual quality in a Pentecostal sense; it captures you in spite of your own limitations. The only way I could describe it would be that I have confidence that I know everything is going to work out all right.

It was no blinding revelation; it came to be through my work with people. For instance, in the town we are calling Mobile there was a large bakery company that would not hire more minority workers. I found a couple of school principals who were very sensitive about their relationships with their hundreds of black students, and I asked if they were willing to suspend the contract for this particular brand of bread. They did and in a couple of days—after feeling at the start it was a noble but losing battle—the company felt the pinch. At the beginning I was even humbly glad to get an appointment to meet with these businessmen. We turned the situation around and they met on our grounds at our convenience. I found that "Name on the door, Bigelow on the floor" didn't mean a thing. With this power of the Spirit I could find their weakness and, if my cause was just, remedy the situation.

Then I was involved for a long time with organizing low-paid blacks who worked in the laundries and schools, also domestics and maids. It was a movement that had larger repercussions outside of our city. Because if these people could successfully organize, similar groups could do the same in other cities, which they did. I worked with blacks and country whites and Indians in a textile mill who were protesting lack of safety conditions, which led to people being maimed regularly. Just to get these people together in the same room would be a problem, but with a common enemy they had to form their own community. As a priest, I wasn't in the negotiations. I was there as a facilitator. But I kept talking to the men, praising them for being together, telling them how great they were to forget the old racial differences. Even though the criticisms came hot and heavy, we could put them aside because we went back to Scripture and found that the Apostles were all workmen, and after the Spirit came to them they continued to mingle with workmen. The only people, the only Apostles in the New Testament that were able to get close to people in some way were ordinary workmen. In fact, so often you would see Christ speaking against the established sterile priesty-type group that had its own sect within a sect. They were often worried about how many candles to use, what color veils, how to wash their hands.

I don't think it's straining the imagination to see the same thing today; I saw it in the South. The chancery office with Monsignor So-and-so in charge of hospitals and someone else in charge of cemeteries or insurance. For the most part very anti-labor people. Men willing to allow hospital or cemetery employees to work for as little as the traffic would bear. Consider how many housekeepers in rectories are not paid well, have no pension plan and no basic sense of job security. And then the pastors are up in the pulpit on Labor Day or at a St. Joseph the Worker Mass and talking about just wages and Pope Leo XIII. But the same pastor would just as soon prefer that his own sexton or housekeeper wasn't listening.

As I got more and more involved in the whole area of civil rights and workers' rights, a concept dawned on me. People had said this can't be done, that can't be done in this backward city; we've tried it before. But by being persistent and believing in the cause and never admitting defeat no matter how many times you're turned down, or turned around, you found things could be done. I'm not talking about having the skill for brain surgery, but I began to feel and believe that whatever came my way I could handle it. It could be worked out successfully. And this only comes in the laboratory of life, with trial and error, and a belief in the Holy Spirit.

I don't want to give the impression that things came easy for me. There was a period of despair when I was in between the older—straight, if you want to use it that way—traditional priesthood and on my way to whatever my life is now—emancipation or new slavery. I think emancipation. There was a period in my early thirties when I didn't know in what direction I was headed, and there were storm clouds all over the place. It was soon after that when my involvement began with the woman whom I would be very close to for the next six years.

It wasn't the crisis where some men saw the new theology that the Council was bringing out and they couldn't reconcile it with their old theology. I didn't even know the old theology. It was more a case of finding my personal identity. I basically liked the direction in which the church seemed to be going, but I still had a personal life, and theology or church didn't touch me that much.

Maybe it was a period of rebuilding, a re-creation, a discovery of what kind of norms I would follow, because you just can't come out of a seminary and find yourself in an affair with a woman—liking it and not feeling guilty—and not wonder what the hell is going on in your life.

What I came to was basically a situation-ethic approach to life. If something I'm doing—like organizing workers—can be reasoned out to be a good thing, why not pursue it? In other situations of life, where there was no cause to be pursued, I had to question, Who am I hurting? I found that this woman grew to love me and I her, and no one was hurt; we were both enriched. Some might say the Man upstairs is being hurt by it. And I say He ought to be able to take care of Himself.

When I'm tired, I sleep. When I'm thirsty, I have a can of beer. When I'm lonesome or need someone to share a joy or sorrow with, I think the companionship of a person of the opposite sex is a most natural desire. I think more priests ought to sweep all the misconceptions and prejudgments out of their minds and start fresh and see where they come out regarding how they should deal with women.

Today's rules of the priesthood deny a man's humanity. Not only in marriage—I'd be an awful husband anyway—but in all relationships with women. How can you possibly say that you are going to get close to someone and yet forgo a most perfect act of expression and love? I know that my loves, especially the six-year one, brought me into life. I experienced the pains and suffering, the loss, and the heartaches that people constantly bring to a priest.

I have a feeling I was called to minister in a unique way. I didn't invent it, but I responded to the things that came along in my life rather than just dogmatically depriving myself because of some rule or regulation by those monks. Without women in my life, I would either not be a priest or I would be a very hollow, ungiving man. I am ready to move with the church; I'm not going to have my faith upset by the discovery of some scrolls in the Middle East that cast doubt on the Gospel of Saint Matthew. I'll take the overall style. George Santayana said he was a Catholic in the sense that he loved the poetry and ceremony and artistry and intrinsic beauty of the church. As far as dogma and details were concerned, he was just not going to worry about them. That's where I'm at; I'll take the overall Christian style.

When as a priest you get involved with a woman for any period of time, you share each other and share mutual dangers. Exposure? Children? Both were very real possibilities to deal with. But in facing those dangers, not running but staying together, there is a special bond.

Exposure is something that any priest would fear, but the overriding desire to be with a person often takes over. It may come as a shock to my priest brothers, but the one woman I was involved with for so long lived with me in the rectory for a time. At first I was alone there and concealing her was no problem. Then another priest moved in, but because we had separate entrances I don't think to this day he knows she was there. I would go downstairs at mealtime and fix something and bring it to the room and share it with her. He must have thought I was a heavy eater. I can remember beautiful times on Sunday mornings when she would help me prepare the homilies for the Masses.

There were times when we'd be talking and wonder, Oh God, did we want to have children! Crazy, this reckless feeling of wanting a child, being ready to follow through on it and do whatever would be needed to take care of the child and our relationship. Most of the time we used various means of birth control, but then there were the times that the moment took over and everything was left up to chance. Abortion we would never consider. And there were times when her period was late. We were half hoping and half—no more than half—in a sweat. We had a code word. It was a girl's name, let's say Mary. And I'd ask her over the phone if Mary had come yet, or she would say Mary was supposed to call two days ago and she hadn't heard from her. Then there were times when her period just wouldn't come. We did worry.

Other men have different reasons for having to consider leaving the priesthood. Mine was the existential reality: Mary just wouldn't come to town. We had said we were willing to take the risk of having children and it looked like it might happen. As the weeks passed, I guess, I got closer and closer to leaving the priesthood; there just didn't seem to be any other decent way out of it. Those were painful weeks, because I didn't want to leave; I was beginning to see a whole new power in the priesthood. Finally Mary, lovable old Mary, came to town. Some months late, but she came.

We talked about the possibility of marriage, but although we shared so many things like a certain lust for life and a sense of humor, it just would not have been a good thing. I don't think race was a factor, for she was black. But if I go back to Mobile and she is still not married, I have no doubt I'll go see her again. What will happen?

That relationship was ideal, one of length and of deep sharing, but I've also traveled through cities in search of a woman; I've cruised bars, not for prostitutes but for companionship. There have been the one-night stands, and I'm not ashamed of those either. I did not tell these women I was a priest; I don't think that was necessary. But I've always tried to maintain a certain quality of truth, of not deceiving these women into thinking that anything more was going to come of it. We knew we were strangers, but we were compatible strangers and we could enjoy each other for a short time and then go our own way.

But even in a short-term relationship more was involved than mere exposure of the body or some animalistic release. I guess I have talked more in bed than most men have. The conversation was to find out about that person and to let her know some of the things that were on my mind. I've always tried to be careful not to engage any woman who was married and still living with her husband; I just couldn't face another man whom I was pushing out of the picture, if only for this one time, and even if I was one of many she might have been with.

Just last month I was walking along Eighth Avenue in New York City and I started talking with one of the prostitutes working that lovely area. It was raining, so we were standing in a doorway and she eventually asked me if I wanted to go with her. I really didn't have any intention of doing anything. She was on the shabby side, so when I told her I had to catch a train (I really did) she said if I didn't want to go with her that she had a friend, pointing to another woman. I said no, if I were to go at all I would go with her. I didn't want her to feel within the framework of her class structure that she wasn't good enough in doing the kind of work she did. I wanted to give her a little pride in her profession.

I think the benefits I've gained from my style of priesthood are many. Take dealing with married couples. Usually I don't have to sit down and convince them I know something about what they're talking about. I don't waste time and tell them that I know; I believe it's reflected, and couples just open right up when they sense they're not talking to some cloistered eunuch. It's not just about sex that people come to a priest, that may be the surface problem. We usually have to continue into the larger realm of intimacy, of people having real trust and feeling for each other—that's what marriages must be based on—and in a sense I had a six-year marriage based on trust and feeling.

I think people can discern what a priest has been through. I think if he's open to them they can sense that he's had to struggle with his life the same way they've struggled with theirs. One thing I surely would never do is turn a person around who comes to me for help and try to be intimate with her. If a woman comes to me in real trouble, needing counseling, and even if the thought was there in the back of my mind: Hey, something could happen here if I nurse it a little bit, I would be misusing the facility of the church. To use a person like that just for my own sexual gratification would leave me a very sorry person.

I've had any number of chances of using women who were beholden to me. When I worked in Mobile most of the workers were women and I could have parlayed my organizer-priest role into a lover's role. I'm sure of that. But there was a trust there and I could not abuse it. I could have hurt people. I could have hurt the cause. If I had been messing around with the women at night that I was marching with during the day, that could have been a powerful weapon against me that could have killed the movement. Even flirting, being overfriendly would have hurt the cause. I was friendly but businesslike, no favorites.

My priesthood has been jeopardized because of the life I've lived. But more because I have been naïve about it. I've taken foolish chances because I was just growing out of boyhood, although chronologically I was in my thirties. I'm better prepared to know what's happening in a relationship now; I'm better prepared not to give false encouragement just to get off on an ego trip and have somebody fall for me. I'm just more experienced in my dealings with women and I can make it healthier for both them and me in the future. And certainly my future will contain women.

But my future is priesthood. One could say I should be a secular bachelor. But the casual bachelor who is a mechanic or a doctor can't touch lives the way a priest can. The priest is still that person who answers the doorbell and is faced with a broken marriage, a broken life, someone who is suicidal, homicidal. There is still something attached to the office of priest that brings people to him when everything else has failed. And he must radiate some kind of empathy, serenity, calmness—things that come from a wellspring of faith that isn't defined in seminary books but by the process of living life. I have lived life and I want to offer it to people. There is no better way I can see to do it than the priesthood.

In many ways I'm a very conventional priest. I genuflect in front of a tabernacle. I believe in the power of prayer. I believe in the need for community. I believe the church has a great potential for change, both a social change of systems and psychological change for people to make them feel that they are worth while. I have the complete conviction that God is on my side as I make preparations to go to South America, not knowing a single word of Spanish, not knowing a thing about the rural setting I'm going into. It's not logical. Perhaps quixotic or fanatical, but it's there. I will be able to reach people and help them in their lives, just by being exposed to them and by living with them. It has worked for me since I've come alive as a priest, so why won't it work for the rest of my life, for as long as I summon the power to make it work?

A writer doesn't sit down and say I'm so inadequate and somebody else should be doing this and I don't know how to do it and let's see if I can find a dictionary. The writer must go in saying, It's got to be done and I'm the one and I'm just going ahead.

Priests have downplayed the role of the Spirit for too long; in the last two decades we've gotten terribly interested in all the theological ins and outs and have forgotten the real power of Christianity. Anticipation has been the biggest problem, lack of abandon. Right now I feel better equipped to take hold of the Spirit, to be used by the Spirit, so why should I even think of a life outside the job that can capture the essence of the Spirit—and that is the priesthood. This is a part of me and even if all my past indiscretions were unearthed, they would have to get some healthy men to drag me out of the church. And then I'd run around the back and bang on the window. But no one has tried to do that, and I have a lot of flexibility to work within the system.

The hassles I've had strengthen the spirit. I was involved with the peace movement in this city in the South that was very dependent on the military budget. Those were the days when you'd get your parade permit and a small band of protestors would march through town and bring out hostilities all out of proportion to the strength that we actually could wield. One afternoon I was waiting in line to get my driver's license renewed, and several men said, Say, ain't you . . . I said no, but they knew me and they dragged me out to the parking lot and bloodied my lip, gave me a swollen face, and tore my clothes. Any one of them—they were husky, healthy characters; one of them was a kind of beach-boy type with bulging muscles and a T-shirt cut off at the shoulders—could have done me in. So I did the bravest thing I could think of at the time. When I got loose, I ran like hell. But I was all the more determined to pursue what I was doing.

All those big involvements, the things that got me into papers and got me known, didn't matter very much when it came time for me to leave. Maybe some of the things people said reconfirmed that I had to be a priest and not just an activist or an organizer.

They said they remembered the time I helped them fill out a

loan application. Found them a place to stay after a house burned down. Stayed with them when they wanted to commit suicide. A person came up to me and said I was there the day before he had an operation and I told him to keep his courage. It was so much help, he told me, and I was embarrassed because I didn't even remember the man. I was a part of those people's lives because I was a priest. They didn't say I was a great force for democracy or workers' rights. It was the personal things, the things that hit just that one person at a time of need.

It may be surprising to mention what happened between the time I left the South and I ended up here. I spent six months in a surburban parish in a middle border state between North and South. Some might consider me the last one to point a finger, but I worked very hard to get the pastor of that church removed. He was a terribly sour, cantankerous person who was so bad that no assistant stayed for more than a year. The people of the church were sick and tired of him, but they didn't know the mechanics of how to get rid of him. I didn't just want to get transferred out and leave those people in the same situation, so I put the right people in the parish in touch with the proper superior in our order. That will take a while, and I am not a person to sit someplace and be long-suffering for someone who shouldn't be there in the first place. He will be removed; I will go to South America and start something entirely different. I felt the spirit was just trampled in that parish, so I have to go to a place where it can flourish.

What I will try to transmit is belief in this idea of destiny; the amazing grace that the Spirit gives was once lost but now it's found. And if I'm authentic, it comes through that amazing grace matters in my life and it can matter in theirs. Ordinary words like hope, love, and faith can have meaning if I can bring people the realization of how these virtues helped in my life. I don't have to hang out the wash; people know.

In my own life I know the Spirit is alive and working in this middle-aged and very carnal body. There are times when I have nothing to say and I have to deliver a speech or a homily, and I know if I can just have ten minutes to go over a section of Scripture I will find something in that text that will come alive. It's not a case of trained eloquence or a command of language, but just the willingness to accept the power. Some could say it's a psychological principle or positive thinking, but my personal fuel comes from that Pentecostal idea of the Spirit, an understanding Spirit. I give God credit—and this is very egotistical—for as much intelligence as I would give myself. I don't believe I would give eternal punishment to a boy for masturbating or a priest for having sex, and I don't think He would either. I believe I would help somebody who was basically trying to work for something he believed in—and so would He.

Would this God sanction the rhythm system of birth control? An animalistic system that says this is the fourteenth day of the month so let's get going. That is mistreating a woman's body. The act of love has nothing to do with the calendar. A couple may have had an argument and then they come back together and the calendar says no. And the calendar says yes in a couple of weeks when the couple has no particular reason other than the fact that they won't be able to do it in another week or so. It's a kind of rape between husband and wife, man the aggressor and woman being told that it's time for her body to be used now. The act of love is an expression that calendars shouldn't control.

I guess I could take criticism of my life seriously but I'd have to see who picks up the first stone. I want to see what kind of sublimation he's had. Sex isn't the only expression; an expensive home with gold ceilings, a good vacation spot, career church climbing. It comes out in many ways.

I do admire the priest who does have that kind of internal discipline where he can control his sexual drives but also doesn't divert them into something selfish. If he is convinced that his is a better way to serve people and serve God, I'd have a great amount of respect for that type of integrity. When we both die maybe he's going to get the higher place in heaven, and I'll get the lower place in hell. Perhaps my way is easier but it has its own particular dangers and hardships. In some ways it's better to be placid in life and not get too involved in the life of another person. I prefer the course of intimate involvement.

[Some months after arriving in South America "Father Killeen" added these lines.]

At first I thought I wanted to do an epilogue to my story but now it seems like more of a preface to a new life as a priest. I hardly recognize the character portrayed in this manuscript, yet it *was* me.

Since coming to my new work I have found a new faith. I am in a small mountain town. I am the priest for a few thousand people. Their love, their spirit of life, their basic innocence, is something I stand in awe of. I shall not betray them! I am a priest forever.

As for the past, well, it happened and it now makes me more understanding of human frailty. Part of that past was a product of too selfish a spirit. I now have different spirit to follow—the Holy Spirit. Somehow I knew it would come. It took fifteen years of effort by many people, but it finally happened. I have received a second ordination. Now I'm the priest I should have been all along. The people did it. The Holy Spirit did it. Praise God!